Stars Shall Bend Their Voices

Poets' Favorite Hymns & Spiritual Songs

Stars Shall Bend Their Voices

Poets' Favorite Hymns & Spiritual Songs

EDITED BY JEFFREY L. JOHNSON

ISBN: 978-1-949039-21-4

Orison Books
PO Box 8385
Asheville, NC 28814
www.orisonbooks.com

Distributed to the trade by Itasca Books
1-800-901-3480 / orders@itascabooks.com
www.itascabooks.com

Cover art: Ekaterina Smirnova, "Cluster I" (watercolor on paper, 52"x40", 2013). Used by permission of the artist. www.ekaterina-smirnova.com

Manufactured in the U.S.A.

ORISON
BOOKS

Follow poet, follow right
To the bottom of the night,
With your unconstraining voice
Still persuade us to rejoice.

–W. H. Auden

A stable lamp is lighted
whose glow shall wake the sky;
the stars shall bend their voices,
and every stone shall cry.

–Richard Wilbur

CONTENTS

INTRODUCTION

Even though the English poet D. H. Lawrence claimed to have dismissed the doctrines of the Christian faith by the time he was sixteen years old, as an adult he confessed that "the hymns which I learned as a child, and never forgot . . . mean to me almost more than the finest poetry, and they have for me a more permanent value, somehow or other."[1] Behind this anthology lies a desire to hear distinguished contemporary poets tell about sacred songs in their lives.

Hymns and spiritual songs preserve religious devotion and faith in musical compositions. If some of the most distinguished contemporary poets agreed to write about hymns and sacred songs, what insights into the pulses of art within the impulses of religion would they identify? What commentaries on religious experience would appear through their reflections? With these questions in mind, poets were invited to name and write about their favorite hymns and spiritual songs.

I chose a diverse group of poet/essayists, from a variety of cultural backgrounds, regions of the country, parts of the world, and stages of their careers. Excellence as poets, in the judgment of critics and their peers, is the quality shared by all of them.

The essays they returned show sympathy as well as antipathy for the hymns in their lives. Some of the poets admit to formative and lasting influence of sacred songs on their secular vocations. They tell how hymns unlocked their muses and freed their voices for vocations as writers.

Each poet interpreted the term "hymn" in his or her own way. Their choices represent a variety of song styles from a number of religious traditions. One poet chose a liturgical hymn from a synagogue service, one chose a liturgical hymn from the Latin Mass. There is an essay on a Baptist hymn of self-examination and personal decision, one on a Methodist missionary hymn, one on a contemporary Catholic hymn, well-known in the current ecumenical climate, and one on a hymn from the eighteenth-century, when great English poets served the English church.

---

1 Emile Delavenay, *D. H. Lawrence, The Man and His Work,* London: Heineman, 1972, pp. 40–42.

There is an essay describing how the music of the Islamic call to prayer reached into a child's room and into her heart, and an essay on the sound patterns and physical movements of Islamic prayer passing from a father to his young son.

There are memories of hymns sung by mothers, reminding readers of the immaculate hymns of Mary and Elizabeth in Luke's Gospel. Two poets took texts without tunes as hymns: a familiar Psalm and an ancient shepherd's miraculous verse of praise that became the mythological headwater of a flood of lyric poems.

The poets' essays turn from literary analyses of hymn texts, and historical reviews of the circumstances of hymn composition, to personal remembrances of soul-expanding experiences of singing, as well as soul-scarring incidents associated with manipulative use of hymns by religious leaders. There are appreciations of spiritual training through singing in the innocence of childhood, within a safe community, and confessions of moments of grief and loneliness when the text and the melody of a hymn brought comfort and encouragement.

The poets tell how hymns can cross-pollenate religions, spread sacred sounds down secular streets, and bring comfort and joy to believers and unbelievers. They tell how hymns served them in moments of darkness and confusion when no other ordered or creative compositions came to mind.

I thank all the poets who responded to an invitation to write about a hymn, even those who declined. These notables returned comments that pointed in directions their essays might have taken.

Donald Hall: "I'm sorry that I cannot do it. I'm eighty-eight, still writing essays, but pretty much know what I can and cannot do. If I could I would write about 'Amazing Grace' but I leave that to Alicia Ostriker! There is a wonderful hymn from a poem by Christina Rosetti . . . . Somebody will want to do it! I'm pretty handicapped and can't go to church anymore. Thanks for including me. It's a great idea."

Ted Kooser: "Though I go to church regularly I have yet to discover a hymn that I especially favor, and I couldn't tell you the titles of the ones that seem familiar to me. I don't much enjoy singing and hymn singing is, for me, mostly going through the motions. I probably wouldn't sing at all if there weren't people standing near me who would wonder why I'm not. So I'm sorry to report that I won't be able to participate in what seems like an interesting idea!"

Gary Snyder: "I grew up a non-Christian, and even though I sang hymns as a professional soprano (before my voice changed) at the Congregational Church in Portland Oregon, they did not touch me except as good language and good music. I do, often, chant Buddhist sutras . . . ."

Jason Denhart, executive director of the Merwin Conservancy, writing on behalf of W. S. Merwin: "Mr. Merwin is the son of a Presbyterian minister whose life-long interest in language began as a very young child, writing hymns for his father's church . . . eighty-some years ago."

Other poets sent notes of support for the project: Elizabeth Alexander, Wendell Berry, Richard Blanco, Ocean Vuong, Carl Dennis, Lynn Emanuel, Tyehimba Jess, Sharon Olds, Mary Oliver, Carl Phillips, Claudia Rankine, and Christian Wiman. I thank all of them. Their attention, however slight, moved the project along.

My deepest thanks to the poets who accepted the challenge to write about a hymn. They became like a temporary congregation to me. I bought their books, read their poems, and learned about their professional lives. Their helpful suggestions, thoughtful conversations, and cheerful and kind communications made editing this book a very pleasant labor.

Jeffrey L. Johnson
Sudbury, Massachusetts

Bismillah rahman rahiim, alhamdulillahi rabbil alamin, aarahma-nir rahim, maliki yaumiddin, iyyaka n'abadu wa-iyaaka nasta'in . . .

KAVEH AKBAR

LEARNING TO PRAY, LEARNING TO WRITE

The first poetry I ever loved was the poetry of prayer, specifically the poetry of Islamic prayer. Everyone knows Muslims pray five times a day, but when my family came to America when I was two, we streamlined our prayer habits. The five daily prayers became one long prayer to say at the end of the day (we were full of these kinds of new-world workarounds—my mother never ate pork except, secretly, in the form of pepperoni pizza). Once every evening, my father would announce it was time for namaz, and he, my mother, my older brother, and I would assemble to do our wuzu (a kind of pre-prayer ablution), then gather in the kitchen or living room or a bedroom to lay out prayer mats and move through the prayers, saying them quietly to ourselves as we cycled through the various postures of devotion.

The prayers for namaz were in Arabic, a language none of us spoke. Farsi, our language, uses the same alphabet as Arabic, but as a member of the Indo-European language family, it's actually more closely related to Portuguese or French. So every day my family gathered together to pray in a language we didn't understand, to repeat these gorgeous, rending strings of sounds together as a way of building direct channels to God. For most of my early childhood, I just moved through the postures along with my family, listening to their whispered words, watching with reverence and fascination as they knelt and cupped their hands in worship. I remember watching my father, the only one of us who was actually raised in Iran, who seemed specifically marked, fluid, holy in these moments. Before I really even understood the point of the praying, I understood that I wanted to be like him. This poem from my first book orbits that idea:

LEARNING TO PRAY

My father moved patiently

cupping his hands beneath his chin,
    kneeling on a janamaz

        then pressing his forehead to a circle
            of Karbala clay. Occasionally
        he'd glance over at my clumsy mirroring,

    my too-big Packers T-shirt
and pebble-red shorts,
    and smile a little, despite himself.

        Bending there with his whole form
            marbled in light, he looked like
        a photograph of a famous ghost.

    I ached to be so beautiful.
I hardly knew anything yet—
    not the boiling point of water

        or the capital of Iran,
            not the five pillars of Islam
        or the Verse of the Sword—

    I knew only that I wanted
to be like him,
    that twilit stripe of father

        mesmerizing as the bluewhite Iznik tile
           hanging in our kitchen, worshipped
        as the long faultless tongue of God.

When I was six or seven, my father decided it was time to teach me to say the prayers on my own. He wrote out the Arabic words using the English alphabet, spelled phonetically, in various colorful inks. He laminated the pages, and every day he and I would spend an hour together sitting on the couch, studying the plastic pages. The line would say "alham dulillahi rabbil alamin, ar rahman ir rahim," and slowly we would make the sounds together, me leaning up toward my father's stubbly lips, blissing in the magical music that came from them. We'd practice saying it all together, moving through the postures right there on the old couch, us both laughing at my forgetfulness, growing tired and hungry. It didn't take long before I had mastered it, could offer fifteen minutes of continuous prayer in this gorgeous, mysterious language. I was so proud—it was the exact same language spoken by The Prophet himself.

The poet Kazim Ali writes, "If prayers can make a place holy, then it must mean there's some divine energy that moves through a human body." I learned from Kazim that the Arabic word *ruh* means both "breath" and "spirit," and this seems absolutely essential to my understanding of prayer—a way of directing, bridling the breath–spirit through a kind of focused music.

This music, this way of hymning directly to God, was my first conscious experience of mellifluous charged language, and it's the bedrock upon which I've built my understanding of poetry as a craft and as a meditative practice. There is no way to divorce my writing life from my spiritual life; that Venn diagram is just one big circle. Whichever Divine I address in my poems today— love, fear, death, family, God, or anything else—first needs to be courted. I learned from an early age language was a way to court the great unknowables, provided it was charged and earnest and true. It's irrelevant if I understand consciously exactly what I am saying, only that I say it urgently enough, speak it with enough beauty of breath and spirit to earn one tiny moment of God's attention.

Takbeerat al-Eid

الله أكبر الله أكبر الله أكبر
God is greater, God is greater, God is greater,

لا اله إلا الله، الله أكبر
There is no God but God, God is Greater

الله أكبر و لله الحمد
God is greater and to God we give thanks

الله أكبر كبيرا
God is greater, He is great

و الحمد لله كثيرا
And we give abundant thanks to Him

و سبحان الله و بحمده بكرةً و أصيلا
And praise be to God and gratitude in the morning and the evening

لا اله إلا الله
There is no God but God

صدق وعده
He has been true to His promise

و نصر عبده
And made His servant victorious

و أعزّ جنده
And made His soldiers glorious

و هزم الأحزاب وحده
And has, alone, defeated those against him

لا اله إلا الله

There is no God but God

و لا نعبد إلا إيّاه

And we worship no God but Him

مخلصين له الدّين و لو كره الكافرون

Faithful to Him even if the faithless hate it

اللّهمّ صلّ على سيّدنا محمد

Prayers be upon our Prophet Mohammad

و على آل محمد

And upon the family of Mohammad

و على أصحاب محمد

And upon the companions of Mohammad

و على أنصار محمد

And upon the supporters of Mohammad

و على أزواج محمد

And upon the wives of Mohammad

و على ذريّة سيّدنا محمد و سلّم تسليماً كبيرا

And upon the lineage of our Prophet Mohammad and peace be upon them

ربّي اغفر لي و لوالديّ

God forgive me and my parents

ربّي ارحمهما كما ربّياني صغيرا

God have mercy on them for they have raised me when I was little

ZEINA HASHEM BECK

WAS THERE A SPEAKER ON THE BUILDING OPPOSITE US?

Whenever I think of takbeerat al-Eid, I remember the curtains of my childhood bedroom—how Mom surprised me one afternoon, saying she had bought me new pink (pink!) curtains. I loved their color and sheer fabric—I could see the glass balcony door behind them, and behind that, the green wooden shutters. When the shutters were open, I could also see the rooftops of the city. And from the rooftops of Tripoli (Lebanon) seemed to rise the takbeerat every Eid morning.

Every Eid morning, I was awakened by the sounds of the prayers from the city's mosques: Allahu Akbar, Allahu Akbar, Allahu Akbar. The word *takbeera* means "to say Allahu Akbar (God is Greater) once," and *takbeerat* is its plural form. Takbeerat al-Eid, which preceded the Eid prayer, repeated Allahu Akbar and added words of gratitude and worship. The chanting usually began on the last night of Ramadan and resumed at sunrise the next day. Though the takbeerat were recited on both Eid al-Fitr and Eid al-Adha, Eid al-Fitr always felt more special for me. The prayers woke me and made me anticipate the un-reversed day—Ramadan was over, Eid was here. After a month of fasting, you drink and think, *I am drinking*. You eat and think, *I am eating*. I always stole a few bites of wara' 'inab from Mom's pot, early in the morning. The night before Eid, Mom cooked the wara' 'inab on a slow fire for hours. The scent of the stuffed vine leaves infused the house, and so did the prayers.

The prayers were a song I'd memorized over the years. As soon as I heard them, I'd start humming along in my head. It wasn't the words that drew me in, as much as the repetition, the rhyming, and the rhythm—an incantation of sorts. These prayers had a beat faster than that of the adhan, which lingered longer on the words Allahu Akbar, and they were carried by a multitude of voices. There was something communal about them, something that said the entire city was celebrating, giving thanks.

The takbeerat sometimes awakened me early enough to catch my father before he went to visit his mother's grave. I put on my new Eid clothes and went with him. I wondered why we visited our dead on the first day of Eid. My parents said it was to reassure them we remembered them, even in our joy. If I didn't catch my father, I went later with my mother to visit her family's dead. In the graveyards, I remember once listening to similar chants; I don't remember the words, but they resembled the Eid takbeerat in their musicality. I was mesmerized by the men with the beautifully orchestrated voices, sitting on the white plastic chairs in the cemeteries, singing hymns—what for, I wasn't sure. The Eid's arrival, and the dead, and God.

God, says the Qur'an, is closer to us than our jugular vein. Though I'm not what one would call a traditional Muslim (I don't get along too well with organized religion), I choose to believe this—that we contain divinity. And when I can't sleep, I sometimes find myself almost instinctively chanting the Eid takbeerat in my head. *Allahu Akbar, Allahu Akbar, Allahu Akbar.* The rhythm and repetition soothe me, and probably the connection to my childhood too. Perhaps what we love best about our favorite religious rituals is what they remind us of.

I don't remember whether or not I could see, from my balcony, one of the speakers projecting the takbeerat across the city. In my mind, I see a speaker on a building opposite us, though I'm not sure it really existed. I call my mother and ask her, "Was there a speaker on one of the buildings opposite us?" She says no, there was nothing visible to us. Talking to my mother, I remember how the takbeerat ended with asking God to forgive our parents, for they have raised us—this was my favorite part of the prayer. My not-so-favorite part was the one that said that the faithful believe, despite the hate of the non-believers. I didn't like this kind of dichotomy, which I realized, even as a child, was part of other religions too. I wanted to exist beyond this "Us" vs. "Them" mentality. On the phone, my mother says, "But if you see it in your mind, then it probably exists." It probably exists, this speaker in my mind in the city behind my bedroom curtain. This speaker, one of many, projecting Allahu Akbar, Allahu Akbar, Allahu Akbar. And I've been saying I'm inhabited by this hymn of calling out and gratitude. I've been saying the music preceded the words—the words seemed to be there merely to fill a longing, to be carried by a choir of voices across a city. But lately, I've been thinking about the words too—about how, even here in the Arab world, Allahu Akbar has become associated with Isis and terrorism, with death and the slitting of throats. Strange that as I'm summoning these Eid al-Fitr memories, as I'm writing this, it's Ramadan. A few days ago, on the eve of this month, there was an attack on a bus of Coptic Christians in Egypt. Yesterday, there was a bombing at an ice cream shop in Baghdad. And look at Syria. So much daily blood. What speakers full of prayer could drown out such grief? What God/Allah is greater/akbar than this? How do I listen? When this month ends, the Eid takbeerat will go up again. And despite what's happening around us (and my secular mind), I try to remind myself of the possibilities inside those words. I try to reclaim the now fear-inducing Allahu Akbar, see it as a reminder: there is something akbar, something greater. We are the speakers, and there is music inside us. A meaning bigger than us exists within us, all of us, no matter what we choose to call it, no matter what hymns we play to conjure it.

Be Thou My Vision

Be Thou my vision, O Lord of my heart;
naught be all else to me, save that Thou art;
Thou my best thought both by day and by night,
waking or sleeping, Thy presence my light.

Be Thou my wisdom, and Thou my true word;
I ever with Thee and Thou with me, Lord.
Thou my great Father, and I Thy true son;
Thou in me dwelling, and I with Thee one.

Be Thou my breastplate, my sword for the fight;
be my whole armor, be Thou my true might;
Thou my soul's shelter, and Thou my high tow'r,
raise Thou me heav'nward, great pow'r of my pow'r.

Riches I heed not, nor man's empty praise;
Thou mine inheritance, now and always;
Thou and Thou only, the first in my heart,
great God of heaven, my treasure Thou art.

Light of my soul, after victory won,
may I reach heaven's joys, O heaven's sun!
Heart of my own heart, whatever befall,
Still be my vision, O ruler of all.

Traditional Irish
Translated by Eleanor Hull (1860–1935)

SCOTT CAIRNS

"BE THOU MY VISION"

I was raised in a family for whom our Baptist church was very much an extension of our family home. While that church was—as I might now parse such matters—a particularly cranky Baptist church, it offered nonetheless a loving community to those *within* it. More importantly, that community offered me a first taste of what I would later call the surrounding love of God.

We sang many hymns together. For the most part, our hymns served collectively to frame what would prove to be the centerpiece of our Sunday services, the sermon that—I now recognize—replaced centuries-old liturgical worship with a something akin to a classroom whose lessons were punctuated with a soundtrack.

The hymns employed within that frame, by and large, fell into two categories—preparation for the sermon and altar call. Most were sentimental and didactic, speaking to the choir—as it were—while pretending to speak to God.

That is also how most of our public prayer served, as well—with the pastor overtly addressing God while more pointedly admonishing the flock.

In any case, one hymn stood profoundly apart from the others, as it seemed to me to be more like prayer than did any other utterance we made; it was, moreover, a prayer that I found myself praying as I sang the words.

That hymn, "Be Thou My Vision," therefore, has always moved me.

I've sung its verses, as I say, since I was a very small child in that very cranky church. In writing this, and thinking back to those days, I'm fairly certain that over those many years I have never managed to sing the hymn in its entirety without—at some point—choking up and falling silent, even as other congregants carried on around me. That is to say that in the course of nearly sixty years, I doubt that I have ever managed to give full voice to the concluding gesture *Heart of my own heart, whatever befall, still be my vision, O Ruler of all.*

Even so, so far as I recall, I have never failed silently to shape those words with my lips while—for all my hope of vision—nearly blinded.

The text comes to us from a 6th-century Irish poem that most of us know in its 1912 English translation by the writer Eleanor Hull; since 1919, Christians have most often sung that poem to the melody of a similarly fetching Irish folk tune.

Something of that hymn's shape—its words and its melody—cuts me deeply. It always has. I'm thinking that this is because the hymn is both a song of genuine worship, and an exceedingly earnest prayer.

Over the past fifteen years or so, my annual pilgrimage to worship and to pray among the saintly monks of Agion Oros—otherwise known as the Holy Mountain of Mount Athos in Greece—has led to my digging more deeply into the foundational practice and language of the early Christian faith. Specifically, certain Greek words have proven useful to my lately developing a more efficacious sense of what we have come to call theology, or God-talk. Chief among those words is θεωρία (theoría), which is to say *contemplation*, or, more to the point of the moment, *vision*.

The Eastern Orthodox Church might be said to be a little stingy in its acknowledging of anyone as a *theologian*. Strictly speaking, our church recognizes but three—just three saints whose names include the epithet *theologian*; they are Saint John the Theologian (also called John the Evangelist), Saint Gregory the Theologian (also called Gregory of Nazianzus, and one of the Cappadocian Fathers), and Saint Symeon the New Theologian. As it happens, each of these men wrote their theologies in poetry, highlighting to some degree the rabbinic understanding that true theology is always parabolic, as the One of Whom we speak extends beyond comprehension, irreducible.

In more recent centuries, recognizing the compelling observation of the 4th-century father Evagrios Pontikos, the term *theologian* has been more generously applied to several dozen others over the centuries; in his *Treatise on Prayer*, Evagrios writes: "If you are a theologian, you will pray truly; if you pray truly, you are a theologian."

Judging from my own experience, one doesn't travel very far in any chosen religious practice without discovering along the way a good bit of paradox to be parsed. One doesn't proceed, I daresay, without often suspecting that one's own disposition may be influencing—even altering—one's perceptions of *what is so*, one's perceptions of the Holy One Who Is, the Holy One we seek. When puzzling over the mystery of our being, one finds plenty of room for interpretive error, even if it is well-intentioned error.

One of the discoveries that led me finally to embrace the Eastern Church was its disposition toward biblical scripture. The church of my youth approached the scriptures as if they were both knowable and reducible to proposition; each verse was approached as a fixed utterance, dictated, word by word, by God to certain men; the scriptures were understood to be God's words precisely, and they were understood to be *the revelation*, as such. On the other hand, Orthodoxy observes that what the God revealed to these men was but a glimpse of Himself, and that those men thereafter employed their own words to offer up what might be better understood as *a witness to the revelation*. That is to say, these writers beheld a mystical vision, and sought to share it by whatever means they could muster.

What we *make* of their textual witness is, of course, yet another matter.

One must appreciate that in any act of reading, the reader is caught in a swirling confluence of what she beholds and who she is, beholding; the reader is ever and unremittingly obliged to bring himself to the mix. All of this brings us to the troubling question along the way: am I seeing something of what is there, or am I projecting my own image upon the text, the scene, the phenomena before me?

In such a circumstance, "Be Thou My Vision" appears as a most efficacious prayer. May it be blessed.

23

A David psalm.

The Lord is my shepherd,
    I shall not want.
In grass meadows He makes me lie down,
    by quiet waters guides me.
My life He brings back.
       He leads me on pathways of justice
           for His name's sake.

Though I walk in the vale of death's shadow,
    I fear no harm,
          for You are with me.
Your rod and Your staff--
    it is they that console me.
You set out a table before me
    in the face of my foes.
You moisten my head with oil,
    my cup overflows.

Let but goodness and kindness pursue me
    all the days of my life.
I shall dwell in the house of the Lord
    for many long days.

Translation by Robert Alter (1935–)

RICHARD CHESS

YOU ARE WITH ME, I AM WITH YOU:
ON PSALM 23, "HOWL, PART III," AND "ARROW & BOW"

I am with you in Rockland
You are with me
I am with you in Rockland
You are with me
I am with you in Rockland
You are with me
You're madder than I am
You are with me
We are great writers on the same dreadful typewriter
You are with me
Where the faculties of the skull no longer admit the worms of the senses
You are with me
. . . in a straightjacket . . . losing the game of the actual pingpong of the abyss
I fear no harm
I'm with you in Rockland
You are with me

*

23. A David Psalm. Part III, "Howl," a Ginsberg poem.

I am not alone, sings the psalmist.

A thousand generations later, I am not alone, recites the mourner. Sandy Hook. Manchester. Paris. Orlando. Columbine. Baltimore. Chicago. Charleston. Her child gone. Her declaration, which she desperately wants to believe, to feel, to know in her heart, her bones, her soul, there in the sanctuary where the funeral for her boy proceeds, followed by the terrible daytime headlight crawl of a drive to the cemetery, the lowering of the plain pine coffin, the first shovelful of dirt striking the coffin's lid, the slow shovelful after shovelful of dirt filling the grave until the hole in the earth is no more a hole, leaving only the hole in her heart.

My life He brings back. Robert Alter's translation. His comment on the verse: "Though 'He restoreth my soul' is time-honored, the Hebrew *nefesh* does not mean 'soul' but 'life breath' or 'life.' The image is of someone who has almost stopped breathing and is revived, brought back to life" (Alter 78).

A mother, her child gone. She almost stopped breathing.

My life He brings back, she recites to herself as she stirs honey into black tea, one mug on the counter on her first morning of living with her nearest dead. Maybe the psalm helps.

*

You are not alone, chants the poet, I am with you in Rockland, Rockland Psychiatric Center in Orangeburg, NY. Wherever I am when I call out to you, Lower Manhattan, Denver, Tangiers, I am with you, declares the poet.

*

But, really, how can that be when I am here and you are there, when we are separated by space, time, existence?

The distance: even an inch can seem like a mile, even a moment can seem like a light year. The exact moment when the distance between self and other, self and beloved, human and divine is felt most acutely—that's when the psalmist, the poet declares, we are together.

A lyric impulse: to deny, to obliterate distance. To make the distance sing.

*

In the face of my foes. Psalm 23. "In an armed madhouse . . . where you accuse your doctors of insanity and plot the Hebrew socialist revolution against the fascist national Golgotha." Part III, "Howl."

*

For the last ten weeks, I've been suffering from the most serious bout of insomnia I've ever experienced. I sleep an hour and a half, then I'm up, fighting with my foe, insomnia, for hours, losing, fearful of the consequences of the sun coming up on a new day of work and other responsibilities, my having slept for only 90 minutes.

Throughout the day, I feel withdrawn, isolated in the fog of exhaustion, my mind slow, my heart unable to respond to beauty, kindness, love.

As part of my daily meditation practice, I often read a few prayers, including the psalm for the day, from the traditional Jewish morning liturgy. Sometimes there's a phrase that calls out to me, and I choose it to repeat internally for the duration of my meditation practice, or I repeat it a few times at the beginning to set an intention, a direction for my morning meditation, returning to it now and then when I find myself lost in thought or fear.

Psalm 23 is not among the texts I regularly read. Let me be honest: I say regularly, but during this period of sleep deprivation, I have not been able to bring myself to read any prayers: they all feel so distant from me, so alien to me, that even reading a few words of them brings little but more pain.

One night, desperate for something to quiet my mind (worrying about work, my responsibilities as new department chair), I recalled a verse from the 23rd psalm, *He makes me lie down by still waters*. The waters of menuchot, deep rest, the kind of rest experienced by God on the seventh day and available to Jews who observe the Sabbath. Well, I mis-recalled that verse, but saying it and visualizing the experience of lying by the waters of menuchot brought me a moment of relief that night. Not sleep, but a brief ceasefire in my war with insomnia.

The next morning, I reached for Robert Alter's translation of *The Book of Psalms*. The language seemed so direct, so clear, so immediate, so fresh, so alive, so contemporary, so useful, so near:

Though I walk in the vale of death's shadow,
I fear no harm,
                for You are with me.

"I fear no harm, / for You are with me."

As helpless, withdrawn, isolated, and utterly alone as my insomnia was making me feel, these two lines comforted me. They became my go-to lines at moments of desperation: desperate to sleep, desperate to feel alive during my waking hours.

You *are* with me.

*

We know what happens before Ginsberg reassures his dear friend Carl Solomon that despite physical circumstances that would suggest otherwise, they are together. In part I of "Howl," Ginsberg famously recounts the nightmarish, outlandish experiences of his countercultural, outcast generation—a generation of "angelheaded hipsters burning for" an "ancient heavenly connection," who in their quest follow intuition and impulse and signs: the "cosmos instinctively vibrated at their feet in Kansas."

In Part II, Ginsberg names the source of his beat generation's suffering: Moloch, that "sphinx of cement and aluminum" that "bashed open their skulls and ate up their brains and imagination."

Then, in Part III, Ginsberg turns to address, console, assure his beloved, locked away for treatment of his "madness."

We don't know the narrative context out of which Psalm 23 emerges. But from the psalm itself, we know this: it begins (verses 1–3) and ends (verses 6 & 7) in the third person, the psalmist speaking *of* his Lord: "The Lord is my shepherd"; "He makes me," "He brings," "He leads."

Then, in the middle, in the heart of the psalm, he speaks directly to God: "You are with me." It is as if suddenly, without warning, the psalmist has become aware of God's presence in his life.

It's a fleeting but crucial moment in the psalm, in the psalmist's consciousness.

From speaking *of*, to speaking *to* without any explicit change in setting or circumstance.

The psalm brings what's distant near.

The psalm enacts a process. The process begins with the psalmist recalling past experiences of God's comfort and protection, which may be a way the psalmist reminds himself that it's possible he'll experience the same again someday. Then, there He is, potently, powerfully, graciously present, consoling, setting a table—in the presence of foes no less—and moistening the psalmist's head with oil and filling his cup to overflowing. A luxurious moment. Then, just as suddenly as God's presence appears, it disappears, but the psalmist's confidence in God's everlasting presence, even when the psalmist may not be aware of it, is reaffirmed: "I shall dwell in the House of the Lord / for many long days."

*

You are with me, I am with you. We breathe the same air, even when we are distant from one another, say a bowshot away from each other.

That's how far apart they sat, Hagar and her child, Ishmael.

Sarah, after the birth of her own son, Isaac, didn't like what she saw, the son of Hagar the Egyptian playing. The son Hagar bore with Abraham. So she ordered Abraham to send Hagar and that boy away, lest he share in Isaac's inheritance. Abraham gave them some bread and a skin of water, and sent them away.

When the water was gone, Hagar could not bear to witness her child's death of thirst. So she left him under a bush and walked away, a bowshot's distance.

Terribly alone and apart, she is overcome by the lyric impulse: she bursts into tears (cries out) or, as contemporary American Jewish songwriter, performer, and poet Alicia Jo Rabins' "Arrow and Bow" has it, into song: "I'll be over here and you stay over there / as long as we both breathe this unforgiving air."

No angel in that air. No god. Suspend the story at that moment, feel your way into it, and you may discover the urgent need to hear someone, some being declare

I am with you (Ginsberg)

You are with me

my little grain of rice, my little blueberry
my fig, my pear, my orange—how you grew in me (Rabins)

In the face of my foes

you bang on the catatonic piano the soul is innocent and immortal it
should never die ungodly in an armed madhouse (Ginsberg)

In the face of my foes

There are twentyfive thousand comrades all together singing (Ginsberg)

You moisten my head with oil

I am with you in Rockland

we both breathe this unforgiving air (Rabins)

*

But the story doesn't end there. God hears the cry of Hagar's boy. And an angel of God calls to Hagar from heaven: "What troubles you, Hagar? Fear not, for

God has heeded the cry of the boy where he is" (Genesis 21:17).

Where he is

My cup overflows

I am with you in Rockland

In the vale of death's shadow

In Rockland

I fear no harm *in Rockland*

For You are with me *I am with you*

That's the story. The song. The poem. The psalm.

Works Cited

The Book of Psalms: A Translation with Commentary. Translated by Robert Alter, W. W. Norton and Company, 2009.

Ginsberg, Allen. "Howl." *Collected Poems: 1947–1980.* Harper & Row, Publishers, 1984.

Girls in Trouble. "Arrow & Bow." *Open the Ground,* 2015, http://www.girlsintroublemusic.com/albums/open-the-ground/.

One Bread, One Body

Refrain:
One bread, one body,
one Lord of all,
one cup of blessing which we bless.
And we, though many,
throughout the earth,
we are one body in this one Lord.

Gentile or Jew,
servant or free,
woman or man, no more.

Many the gifts,
many the works,
one in the Lord of all.

Grain for the fields,
scattered and grown,
gathered to one, for all.

John Foley, 1978–

KATE DANIELS

ONE BREAD: ONE BODY: ONE LOVE

I.

I grew up in the authoritarian framework of the Southern Baptist Church, and when I was a girl, my understanding of the world depended upon a cooperating pair of dualities that functioned in my everyday life almost as actual people: a teacher and a cop.

The Simplicities were teachers, charged with passing along a very simple, either/or set of rules. Do this. Don't do that. They concretized themselves in God's word, the Bible.

The Authorities were cops. Guard dog-like, they dominated every aspect of my life as a child, and assumed physical reality in the adults who surrounded me in my family and my church. Their job was to enforce the rules.

You could say it was not a capacious theology, dominated, as it was, by a single subject: sin. Capital S. Capital I. Capital N. Past, present, and future sin. We were born in sin we could never slough off. We were constantly being caught in the act of sin. We were relentlessly reminded to refrain from sin. Real life sometimes seemed hardly more to me, in those early years of childhood, than constant, ongoing examples of real sin coupled with apparently unlimited opportunities for potential sin. Church was a place where it was never possible to forget how narrow was the road to God's grace, and how unlikely it was that a sinner such as I would be able to follow it to the ultimate reward. From the pulpit emanated a constant, didactic beat; its purpose was to remind us that sin was all around. Even now, I can hear the syncopatic, anapestic rhythm that every Baptist preacher I ever listened to belted out. In my head, it translated into something like tom-tom drums: SIN - sin - sin // SIN - sin - sin // SIN - sin - sin . . .

Although this doctrine had produced generations of simplehearted, loving, hardworking Christian people in my family, it was, for me, an unfortunate frame of religious belief to have been born into. In many ways, I was my family's natural product: a devout and God-loving child. But I had the sensitive, language-oriented temperament of a future poet. Like many people who express themselves through the arts, I was introverted and private with a highly reactive brain chemistry that rendered me vividly imaginative, but left me overly sensitive to impingements. Exposure humiliated me. Disapproval scourged me. Fear flayed me. Beauty flattened me. Sitting in church, I felt bathed in klieg lights that shone nonstop on all my inadequacies. By the time I was in school, I had managed—through the offices of reading and writing—to secure a small internal privacy, a kind of psychological bolthole that saved me from being overwhelmed with self-hatred. In this cloistered place, I regularly secluded myself to write poems and stories, and to practice a completely private prayer life that tended towards the animistic. I longed—without being aware that I longed—for a way to worship aesthetically, to express my complicated and passionate feelings about God in modes of communication not ordinarily used in everyday life. Outside, the church preached separation and hierarchy. But inside, God felt all of one piece, a huge, unruly front of affect that moved through me like weather, all-consuming and mysterious. In church, where I was obliged to sit still and affectless through long worship services, all dressed up and cramped inside "Sunday clothes," I could not make the inside and the outside fit together.

My family attended services at a venerable old Baptist church founded in 1814. Its architecture conspired to enforce the unconscious matrix of dualities that ruled my spiritual life. Sunday School—all fun with Kool-Aid and cut out Jesuses—was held in its own, separate building. There, we sang boisterous rounds of "Deep and Wide" and wailed out "Jesus Loves Me," absorbing a child's version of the Word. Afterwards, we tried to settle down, walking across the grounds to the church proper: tall-steepled and brick. Inside, the sanctuary was formal, hushed, symmetrical—all red velvet, stained glass, dark wood. There, we children stifled ourselves, or were stifled by the Authorities. Church was serious business filled with grownups, stiffened up in their Sunday clothes and wearing somber expressions. The pastor and his deacons moved among us: tall, dark, and remote, infused with silent power. Like the cops they represented to me, they directed traffic in the parking lot and pointed out where to sit inside. They handed us our bulletins, walked down the aisle with the pastor, collected our money, and—once a month—distributed the chrome trays of grape juice and cubed loaf bread that represented the body and blood of our Lord. The men were animate, powerful figures who dominated church services while the women worked behind the scenes, arriving at worship embedded within clutches of children over whom they exercised knuckle-rapping, ear-pulling control. Their job was to keep our bodies still and our voices silent as we absorbed the dictates the Authorities both represented and enforced.

II.

Deacon Jacobs was one of the Authorities. A tall, powerful man, he was a car mechanic with permanent rinds of black-green oil around his knuckles and fingernails that caused my mother to draw back slightly when he passed the collection basket down the pew to us. His daughters were friends of mine, but his only son had stricken him by refusing to be drafted into the US Army for deployment to Vietnam. Dale, Jr. had grown his hair, burned his card, and fled (it was rumored) to Canada. This was not only a deep rejection of his family's faith and way of life, but—practically speaking—a mortification for Deacon Jacobs among the congregation for whom he was supposed to be a model. Something clearly had gone wrong, and—in the parlance of our church—he needed to get himself right with Jesus. He was a good man, I think, and I am sure he did that spiritual work in private, and that he must have struggled mightily as he worked his way through the crisis of faith and family. That our church community required him to perform this expiation in public, however, was horrifying to me, and I have never forgotten the Sunday that Deacon Jacobs staggered up the aisle, weeping and groaning aloud. I couldn't *bear* the exposure of it, and found it shameful that God—even our God who always had his belt at the ready—could treat a person like that. I spent my last years in the Baptist Church with my head buried in the Old Testament, trying to forge a literary escape from the prison house of a theology to which I was unsuited. I could not make myself happy or at home in a worship practice that felt so invasive, and that replaced my richly imagined God the Creator with an intrusive, vengeful deity that required mortifying public performances to remain in good grace.

III.

Sometimes, music—the great old-time gospel hymns of the Baptist church— provided a temporary respite. My paternal grandmother was born in 1898 on a farm in Tidewater, Virginia. Generations of her family were buried in the same Baptist churchyard in New Kent County. Although my Gran was only minimally educated, she had an undeveloped, natural ear for music. One of my earliest memories is sitting alongside her in a metal glider on the front porch of her small home just off Route 1 in Southside Richmond. Her life was hard, and her faith was simple. Picking out hymns on an old guitar, and singing along in a quavering, top-of-the-register voice seemed to help her cope. It was she who first introduced me to the hymns I would later sing in church: "Bringing in the Sheaves," "Rock of Ages," "Amazing Grace," "Just as I Am," "What a Friend We Have in Jesus."

Because it made her happy, my younger brother and I learned to sing my grandmother's hymns. Later, we sometimes performed as a duet in church on Sundays. On those occasions, my father drove into town to fetch my Gran and bring her to services so she could hear us, dressed up in our Sunday best, huddled together over a shared hymnal in front of the church. I am sure my spirit must have soared a bit as my brother and I combined our voices in our sibling harmonies, singing the hymns our grandmother had taught us. What I remember of those occasions, however, was the quaking fear of making a mistake—up there in full sight of God, the pastor, and the congregation—and the punishment that would surely follow.

IV.

I was ten years old, in February 1964, when I first attended a Catholic Mass, taken there in a passel of kids by my mother's friend, Trula, whose family we were visiting in Florida. Trula was the only one of the four adults who went to church that morning, so I must have had the choice of whether to go along or not. All these decades later, I can't recall why I went, and it seems strange to me now that I would have chosen to attend church on a rare Sunday when I might have skipped it, entirely guilt-free. For whatever reason, or through the grace of a merciful god, I *did* go, and it changed my life.

Fifty years later, I can still recall many details of that first Mass—what the church looked like (palm trees outside, traditional cruciform inside), where we sat (second pew on the left), how the light fell in through the stained glass, the intriguing fact that all the women and girls wore hats or bits of lace on their heads. I felt as if a thirst was being quenched, and I drank in those details over and over as I sat uncomprehendingly through the Mass with its unfamiliar language (Latin), its large inventory of paintings and sculptures and candles and flowers, and the heavy scent of incense that the priest had flung toward us as he processed down the aisle. It weighted down the air we all breathed in together.

Over and above these intriguingly different visceral details of a new kind of worship, there was something I couldn't have described then. Nevertheless, it was what imprinted me most deeply of all: privacy in worship. For the first time, I felt completely safe in church. Rote prayers were either silent or recited together—not improvised as they were at home. Worshippers sat and stood together, as we did, but they also periodically moved their bodies in interesting ways, genuflecting, thumping a gentle fist over their hearts, bending down, all in a noisy herd, to lower the kneelers. In my church, we kept our hands in our laps and to ourselves. But at Mass, people's hands moved in all kinds of interesting ways, making the sign of the cross, fingering rosaries and crucifixes. Sometimes they raised these things—which looked like jewelry to me—up to their lips and kissed them! As imaginative as I was, I had never imagined *kissing* in church.

The elders of this church were all men just as they were in mine. But these men were different, androgynously clad in long gowns instead of suits, and adorned with gold sashes and tasseled belts. They flung about pots of incense, washed their hands daintily at the altar, and were served by a retinue of altar boys. They did not thunder at us, but murmured softly in a foreign language, almost as if we weren't necessary to what was going on. For the most part, they left us alone with our thoughts. Toward the end of that first Mass, I was stunned when the entire congregation rose up and went forward to receive the Eucharist, to claim for themselves the gift. Back home, we waited passively for one of the deacons to pass us our homely bit of Wonder Bread and single sip of Welch's grape juice. Here, in this new church, the bread was a thin and elegant wafer, drawn forth from a gold chalice, and the blood was bitter-tasting real wine.

V.

After that first Mass, I continued to attend Baptist services with my family. With a new model of worship in my mind, however, I chafed at its familiar strictures. By the time I was fourteen, I found more and more excuses to skip church. At school, I filled in part of the gap by singing in choruses where much of our repertoire consisted of 18th-century sacred music. For most of what remained of adolescence, I prayed privately, I sang, and I carried around in my head all those private feelings about God that did not fit any of the contexts which my life at that time offered me. I often revisited in my imagination the experience of that first Mass where I felt both privately held and publicly affirmed while worshiping. In my head, I sometimes held up, in a measuring manner, the two experiences: private and protected from exposure at the Mass, and the traumatizing memory of poor Deacon Jacobs as he staggered down the aisle, publicizing his misery.

And then, just as the radical reorientations of Catholic worship instituted by the Second Vatican Council began to be apparent in the American church, I went off to college in Charlottesville, Virginia. There, I ended up in a suite of girls, many of whom were cradle Catholics from the Northeast. They astonished me by voluntarily attending Mass every Saturday evening. Weekly

Mass was built into their lives in a casual, comfortable way. It was something they did for themselves as much as, if not more than, something they did out of obligation. To say the least, this was an unusual attitude for college students in the early 1970s, and I began to walk out with them on Saturday evenings to see what kind of church evoked such affectionate loyalty. That is how I came to the "new" Catholicism—a phenomenon that astounded me right from the start. I found it housed in a church building unlike any I had ever seen: a "church in the round." It was a circular brick building, topped by a simple cross, and served by Dominican priests. To enter, you walked across an elevated walkway where a larger than life-sized sculpture of St. Thomas Aquinas had been installed. He was made entirely of chrome bumpers salvaged from junked cars. Never had I seen such art in church: discernibly figural, but also abstract. My nascent English major's mind went to work on it immediately, finding provocative the idea that a saint might be soldered together from junk. Here was something different: a church that encouraged a person to think for herself about who a person was, and what it took to become a saint.

These Saturday evening guitar Masses astonished me with their informality. They quickly obliterated my old ideas about attending church: dressing up in uncomfortable clothes, disciplining myself to sit still and impassive through the service with its keening soundtrack of organ music. At St. Thomas, many of the students arrived with bare feet and patched blue jeans. They sat cross-legged on the floor before Mass, playing guitar, chatting and laughing. Sometimes if you arrived early, a gallon bottle of cheap wine might be passed around. Afterwards, we gathered in the vestibule for potluck suppers. I wouldn't care for much of that now, but back then, God-hungry, and trying to find my way into a new form of worship, I was enthralled by the invitation to be myself, private and dressed down.

It would not have been in this church where I first heard "One Bread, One Body" (because it was not written until after my time there). But my early experiences of Catholic worship—first, as a child in a traditional Latin Mass, and later as a college student attending a revisionary, hippie-style Mass in the round—set the stage for my encounter with this very simple hymn which has come to mean more to me than any other.

VI.

Like the new church architecture-in-the-round, "One Bread, One Body" comes directly out of the Second Vatican Council. Under its directives to maintain "noble simplicity" in all Church matters, but with permission to respond to the "local traditions" of individual parishes, Catholic worship radically reimagined itself. Priests turned around to face their parishioners, women removed their head coverings, and vernacular languages replaced the worldwide use of Latin. In St. Louis, a group of young Jesuit seminarians collaborated on liturgical music for a new era. They modeled their hymns on popular forms like folk music and easy listening, and composed them for acoustic guitar. Accessible, musically stripped down, and closely tied to Scripture, "One Bread, One Body," composed by John Foley in 1978, is a good example of the work of the St. Louis group, as they came to be known. Together, they created a series of accessible new hymns that have become iconic elements of Catholic worship in our time: "Be Not Afraid," "The Cry of the Poor," "Though the Mountains May Fall," "Earthen Vessels," "Here I Am Lord."

The scriptural reference of "One Bread, One Body" is from 1 Corinthians 10:16-17:

> The cup of blessing which we bless, is it not the communion of the blood of Christ? The bread which we break, is it not the communion of the body of Christ? For we being many are one bread, and one body: for we are all partakers of that one bread.

It's a short hymn with a haunting tune and simple lyrics that barely proceed past the scripture.

Here is the refrain:

> One bread, one body,
> one Lord of all,
> one cup of blessing which we bless.

And we, though many,
throughout the earth,
we are one body in this one Lord.

Made mostly from nouns and prepositions, and the verb *to be*, it emphasizes its simplicity by confining its lexicon to one and two syllable words. If there is an adjective present, it is the word *one*, used repetitively to modify the bread, the body, the blessing, the Lord. It's hard to miss the point: One is the answer. One word, one syllable, one cup, one Lord, one church, one body of Christ which encompasses the entirety of humanity even as it cradles each of our individual selves.

But this simplicity is also baffling. The image center of the hymn is its "cup of blessing"—easy enough to understand and imagine. Handed to us, we drink from it. But what does it mean for us, as mortals, to bless the God-given cup of blessing? Reciprocity of grace was not anything I ever thought about in the top down theology I learned in early life. Squashed and fearful of my own sinfulness, I don't think it ever occurred to me that I, myself, might have it within me to confer a blessing upon another. One of my favorite parts of the Right of Christian Initiation of Adults was the ritual in which my sponsor—an ordinary human like myself—blessed me over and over, anointing my head and heart, my hands and feet with oil.

From the first time I sang this hymn in Mass—it would have been in Baton Rouge in the 1980s—I felt mystically drawn into something larger than myself—a delicious vastness within which I experienced myself as part of a whole, but also decidedly separate. I call this now the Body of Christ.

There are so many ways to God. "One Bread, One Body" has helped me to understand that. My family members found salvation and sustenance in forms of worship that constricted my spirit—the alien, future poet spawn whom they had given birth to. While their spirits soared under plain white steeples and inside stripped-down sanctuaries where legions of dark-suited men transmitted narrow interpretations, mine withered, compacting under the pressure, into a smaller and smaller space. The joy my loved ones found there was inaccessible to me. Nevertheless, we remain together in loving communion within the Body of Christ, a fact I celebrate whenever I sing "One Bread, One Body."

VII.

The internet can be so disorienting, so weird. But I sure do love it. On Sunday mornings when I can't go to Mass, I like to watch You Tube videos of "One Bread One Body." The iconic version in its original guitar form is the one that pops up most often, but there are lots of variations. A gorgeously gowned Methodist choir all lined up at the front of their church in Minnesota. Ordinary parish Masses all over the world. An all Filipino choir at Holy Rosary Church in the middle of the desert in Qatar, performing a gorgeously harmonized version. Watching the different interpretations of this simple hymn with its haunting, deconstructed melody and its unpretentious lyrics is *always* a moving experience for me. When I can't get to church, I give myself a kind of private Mass through the technological marvel of online music—its own kind of blessing.

One of the videos of "One Bread, One Body" that I particularly love is filmed from behind the altar at Epiphany Church in Gramercy Park, Manhattan. It's first communion. The camera captures the priest's familiar movements as he prepares the gifts. Over his shoulder, just past the altar, you can see the congregation stretching out. The new communicants fidget excitedly in the front rows, and behind them, the rest of the flock presents a panorama of the Catholic Mass' peculiar mixing of the sacred and the secular. Born a Southern Baptist, I still marvel at it. While the priest is overseeing the Eucharistic miracle of transubstantiation, the people may be barely paying attention. They're whispering and waving to each other, or sending a clandestine text message from a phone concealed in a pocket, or writing in their checkbook the amount they just dropped in the offertory basket. An astounding number of congregants are constantly flowing in and out of the sanctuary. Regardless, everyone's body language is casual and free. Some worshipers arrive late, many leave early. The vestibule, which you can see at the rear of the frame, is packed with these late arrivers and early leavers. At the back of the church, a standing woman rummages at length in a huge shoulder bag, and over on the side, a man sits with his arms clasped behind his neck, elbows soaring out from his body like butterfly wings. Any number of women have arrived at Mass in spaghetti-strapped sundresses, exposing cleavage and bare backs. There are men trussed up in suits and ties, and men at ease in shirtsleeves. The space inside the Catholic Mass for human beings to be what they are—human, necessarily imperfect and messy—continues to compel and move me. Sometimes the juxtapositions still make the suppressed Protestant inside me rise up, pursing her lips. I no longer do this with judgement, I'm glad to say, but with a kind of inner laugh. With relief. This is what "One Bread One Body" represents for me—a praise song for a God who looks at us all with a forbearing and humorous nature. Who blesses us all, and leaves us alone much of the time to work it out by ourselves. Sometimes mistakes are made, but they are never fatal though they may seem so in the short run. For God's time is not our time, and our Catholic faith offers us a multitude of ways—an overflowing cup of blessings—to correct our failings.

Once, attending Mass in Durham, North Carolina, alone with my three young children, two of them still in car seats, all hell broke out between them over a Ziploc bag of cheerios that had been consumed earlier than I'd calculated. Struggling to quiet them and restore order to our caterwauling corner of the pew, and horribly anxious about the raucous spectacle we were making, I was distracted by a touch on my arm. An older woman was leaning toward me, gesturing towards my atrociously misbehaving offspring. She looked very much like one of the church women of my childhood, all dressed up in Sunday clothes, and I tensed up, anticipating the rebuke I sensed was coming. Then I saw she was smiling. To me, it was a Catholic smile. "Don't worry, sweetie," she said. "We're just glad you're here." The relief that swept through me at her words was a giant cup of blessing. I gulped it down. In my head, I blessed her back. When I was able to tune into the Mass again, the gifts were being prepared, and the parish music minister was instructing us to turn to #498 in *Glory & Praise* so we could sing, together, "One Bread, One Body."

Great Is Thy Faithfulness

Great is Thy faithfulness, O God my father;
there is no shadow of turning with Thee.
Thou changest not, Thy compassions, they fail not;
as thou hast been, thou for ever will be.

Great is Thy faithfulness!
Great is Thy faithfulness!
Morning by morning new mercies I see.
All I have needed Thy hand hath provided.
Great is Thy faithfulness, Lord unto me.

Summer and winter, and springtime and harvest,
sun, moon and stars in their courses above
join with all nature in manifold witness
to Thy great faithfulness, mercy and love.

Pardon for sin and a peace that endureth;
Thine own dear presence to cheer and to guide.
Strength for today and bright hope for tomorrow,
blessings all mine, with ten thousand beside

Thomas O. Chisholm 1866–1960

KWAME DAWES

"GREAT IS THY FAITHFULNESS": A MEDITATION

When faith is married to art, something visceral happens in the engagement with the art. In some ways, one may easily suspend questions of artistic merit in the interest of sentiment, for faith, at least in the way that I have encountered it, has been marked most significantly by something closer to sentiment, the emotion and passion of the thing. I have encountered the lyrics of hymns and songs that have impressed me with their cleverness, their wit, and their capacity to use language in intellectually engaging ways, but such songs tend not to be among the ones that draw out something deeply emotional and sustaining in me. In this sense, I have to suspect that melody, the manner in which a musical composition creates a sense of satisfaction and affirmation, might have a great deal to do with the unconscious pleasure and uplifting that makes me return to certain songs and not others. I realize also that the idea of a favorite hymn is inevitably subjective, and that subjectivity is shaped by the way that music makes us. While I am sure that music has had this peculiar effect on human beings since the beginning of time, it is hard for me to ignore the phenomenon of popular music and the remarkable technological developments of the 20th century that made music ubiquitous—constantly present, capable of insinuating itself into settings that would seem completely incongruous to the very music we are listening to—and so, ultimately, paved the way for music to become one of the key defining factors of how we associate memory with experience.

More crudely put, I suppose, the 20th century has made it possible for most people to speak of having a "soundtrack" to their lives. The very idea of a "soundtrack" of course, owes its existence to the film industry and the ways in which it has given us this working vocabulary through the actual product of the film. In film, we have managed to view a process whereby music serves as the accompaniment of experience—and for the most part, this music presents itself not as a conscience presence in the lives of the characters in the film, but as an orchestrated interpreter of experience, a sound that triggers feeling by association. Those of us who have encountered this phenomenon have likely imbibed this associative process without even thinking just how much it has shaped us. So much so, we have likely found ways to imagine ourselves moving through the world in the way that film enacts that movement for the narratives of the lives of characters we encounter in films.

I suspect that for most of us who have lived with the presence of the great technologies of the 20th century—namely the record player, the radio, the film, the sound system, the various vehicles by which music is given to us—it is possible for us to hear a song or a tune that may have absolutely no obvious connection with an emotion, and to be moved by the song in seemingly contradictory ways. When I, for instance, hear the reggae song "Breakfast in Bed," I find my throat swelling up with a quality of nostalgia and melancholy that I associate with uneasy days in Jamaica spent as a twelve-year-old, worried about death. Jamaica was still a new place to me, and I was still learning the patwa language, but I was also starting to think of myself as mortal, as capable of dying. This jaunty, sweet reggae song, full of sexual innuendo, had nothing to do with death, and yet that is the association I make each time. There are, no doubt, better examples. Music does have this peculiar quality of engaging the subconscious, and I am quite sure that there have been great studies of this phenomenon worth reading and examining. But that is not my goal here. I am more interested in the ways in which this peculiar quality has shaped my choice of "favorites" when it comes to spiritual songs.

I should briefly explain that I did not convert to Christianity until I was about seventeen years old. And I did not proclaim this publicly until I was eighteen. I did not become part of a church, and so I did not have the kind of grounding in church existence that many of my friends have had in their lives. My first years as a Christian were directly associated with my years as a university student searching for meaning and an understanding of the troubling questions of life. I was studying the so-called great philosophers even as I was contending with my faith. I was deeply consumed by the remarkable and defining phenomenon of reggae music and Rastafarianism, as I contended with faith. My teachers of my faith were all relatively young people, largely maverick

Christians who had joined the Charismatic movement, in many cases as acts of rejection of the traditional Christian church in Jamaica. I came to the faith through a tough and intense commitment to the notion of "prove it to me"—a fierce apologetics that seemed to fire these young "rebels." They were rejecting both Babylon and its lackeys as well as Rastafarianism and its presumed heresies. They were skeptical of colonialism and American imperialism, and they were equally bothered by the presumed atheism of Socialism. They were believers of the book who fully trusted that existing in the Bible and available for understanding through the guidance of the Holy Spirit who actually spoke to us, was a truth that they could, we could, come to an understand. I say this to explain that the young man that I was during those days could have been easily confused with a radical leftist who still held to deeply Pentecostal views. I was open, questioning, hungry, and in profound ways, I was being guided by the fire of revelation. Essentially, my growth was characterized by first having encounters of inexplicable passion and the supernatural, and then spending time trying to understand their efficacy through a careful and rational studying of the Bible. I was at once, then, filled with the brokenness of my incapacity to obey the tenets of holiness, and with my deep need for godly forgiveness and freedom. Heady, complicated, and exciting, my early years of faith still shape how I view the world today.

When asked to write about a "favorite" hymn, I went through a list. Typically, I began to think of lyrics, of the poetic capacity of the songwriters, and I began to ask myself which of the hymns I know really impress me with their art. Inevitably I found myself turning to the Psalms-inspired songs simply because I have long been taken by the lyric power of the Psalms, their beauty, their artistry, their complexity, their raw emotion, and their capacity to capture the reaching for a divinity that is intimate, both present and yet distant and overwhelming. There is something deeply human about the Psalms. One of the choruses I would sing to myself while making an early morning pilgrimage into the hills of Jamaica to pray was a rendering of one such psalm (Psalm 5).

Give ear to my words, Oh Lord,

Consider my meditation.
Harken unto the voice of my cry,
My king and my God,
For unto Thee will I pray,
My voice shalt thou hear in the morning.
Oh Lord in the morning
Will I direct my prayer
Unto Thee and will look up.

I would repeat this song again and again, until, filled with a sense of confidence and assurance in what I would understand to be "the presence of God," I would pray freely. The song is anchored by a connection with the moment—the idea of praying in the morning. This may sound terribly obvious, but there is something about singing the words written by an ancient that reminds us that facing a new morning is one of those instances of human consistency that places us among all humans in life as well as in death. This is the secret trigger for me. It always was the trigger. David (or whoever wrote those words) stood in his country and wrote a song as the sun came up, and I, thousands of years later, am finding the same inspiration and meaning in those words, while I face my morning. This strikes me as humbling, reassuring, and beautiful.

The lyric has something to do with this, but so does the melody. It is hard for me to explain the way in which the melody of this song affects me, but I can say that my body responds well to the fact that it covers a tonal range that comes close to straining my vocal capacity (especially if I begin in the wrong key) without causing great alarm. The pleasure is that for most of the song, there is the sweet place of ease in the melody, and as with the best choruses, it rounds itself beautifully to closure, but begs for repetition. One can tell when a chorus will become popular. If it lends itself to the round, it tends to be appealing. This small chorus has that splendid capacity because it begs us to return to the beginning again and again. And the repetitive nature of each narrative line allows us to imagine someone following behind to create the seemingly accidental "harmonies" of sound and melody that we get with the best of rounds.

Yet, the song I have chosen is "Great Is Thy Faithfulness." It is a "classic" hymn in the sense that it is in the style of 19th-century hymns in its language and musical style. The history of that song has never shaped my reaction to it. Until I decided to write this piece, I had never even thought for a moment about who wrote the song, where it came from, and what it might have meant to the person who composed it. I selected it because when asked to pick songs for any important occasion in my life and in the life of my family, I have always picked this song. I have always picked it because it has consistently articulated my sense of gratitude for the things that have gone well in my life and in the lives of those that I love. It is fundamental and basic in its doctrine of salvation. If I claim to be a Christian, which I do, then this song does the work of laying out the character of devotion and submission to God. It presents the core argument of the faith, and it lends itself to repetition. It is a hopeful song. In the manner in which I remember it, the final verse is always joyful especially when it moves toward the affirmation of the chorus. And musically, the chorus is perfectly memorable. Indeed, the way that it rises to its triumphant repetition, and the sweet spot of "thine hands have provided," which begs for harmonies of rich depth and complexity, makes it hugely affirming and uplifting, as great hymns should be. The "argument" of the song is basic. As an apologia, it presents the case for the claim that the chorus presents: "Great is Thy faithfulness, Lord unto me." Each verse is an argument, and the chorus affirms that argument. So that when the final verse declares, "blessings are mine with ten thousand besides!" it makes sense to then fall into the almost militant and joyous declaration, "Great is Thy faithfulness!"

It is a curious thing to me that I did not select a song that has demonstrated a flexibility such that it has been allowed to be rendered in different musical styles that mean a great deal to me. There is no Reggae version of the song that stands out to me, nor is there a High Life version of the song that sticks in my mind. Oh, I am sure that it has been rendered in many styles, but almost always, in Jamaica, the song is rendered in that deeply Victorian style, slow, steady, with the sense of the cathedral rising around it. And yet most of the times I have sung this song, it has been in the anti-cathedral setting of small groups, impromptu gatherings, outdoors, and in the world of the Charismatic movement that raised me in Jamaica. In other words, I encountered that song during periods when the "hits" of worship were modern choruses, very contemporary and almost in defiance of the rituals of the established church. And yet, significantly, our leaders would somehow remember this gem, and in this new space, the song would assume great meaning because our ability to find in it the doctrinal and emotive familiarity of our faith proved to be central to its power and meaning. In a time when the great doctrine of the time among Charismatics was "what new thing is God doing?", this old song would both unsettle us and move us for its age (and hence its unexpected freshness), its relevance, and its beauty.

I chose this song because somewhere in our lives, my wife and I agreed that "Great Is Thy Faithfulness" is our hymn. There is a difference between what might be her hymn and what might be my hymn, and what proves to be our hymn. For instance, whenever I purchase a new pen, I almost always write the following words down: "When I survey the wondrous cross." I wouldn't call this a favorite, but I would call it a song of importance to me, for it spells out with explicit clarity and some skill the fundamental tenets of Christian salvation. But "Great Is Thy Faithfulness" is the song that is easily incorporated into all communal occasions, especially family occasions. Part of the ritual of the life that my wife and I have established as a family has been the affirmation of the various ways in which we have seen grace in the providence of our lives. We have had hard times, times of need and want, times where death lurked in the shadows, times when we did not know what lay in the future—times, in other words, when we felt out of control. As immigrants we have experienced that the massive sense of stepping blindly into the unknown has characterized who we are and what we do, and so the faithfulness of God has been something we have easily felt the need to express gratitude for. This hymn works for so many occasions. When my father died suddenly and tragically, the question was what to offer as songs for his funeral. My father was a Marxist, and while he never claimed atheism as a dogma, I still remember him quipping, "The ancestors

I know, but J. Christ esq., I do not know," or something to that effect. But his children had all managed to reconcile their cultural socialism with a genuine and perhaps radical faith. My mother was a longstanding Catholic who had developed a more evangelical bent in time. And so we were fully aware that the funeral was both for him and for us. "Great Is Thy Faithfulness" made the list. It also made the list of songs for my wedding with Lorna, and Lorna and I have shared this song in any environment that has warranted the expression of who we are in the world in terms of our spiritual sense of the world and the grounding of our lives.

This song offers some of the key qualities for that curious combination of prayer and congregational affirmation. Theologians probably have a term for this, but in my mind, it is especially telling that some songs lend themselves entirely to almost closed prayer, while others speak in communal terms such that the "audience" for the song is the rest of the congregation. In this song, the audience is, first and foremost, God. The song addresses him. And the speaker is a singular speaker—it is the "I," the "me." Hence the song makes sense to the evangelical mind—the mind that seeks to articulate an intimacy with the deity to whom one speaks. Yet the shared sentiments of the song, the shared awareness of what God's faithfulness has ensured, is decidedly one of the critical ways in which the song becomes a communal one, one in which all the singers are at once affirming a deeply personal relationship with God and at the same time, a communal affirmation of that relationship with those within earshot.

For a self-proclaimed roots man, a man who is acutely aware of the complexities of post-colonialism; and more than that, for a man whose embrace of Christianity was delayed for years because of the deep struggle I had intellectually and philosophically with the history of Christianity and its relationship with colonialism and slavery; and further, for a writer who has been explicit that reggae music's capacity to engage what Kamau Brathwaite calls Nation Language, and to affirm an African sense of culture and identity, something does seem almost contradictory in this impulse toward a song that employs archaisms and a musical style and cadence that are decidedly Eurocentric.

The best I can offer is that those characterizations of self are as always limited and rarely reflect the contradictions and complications of our lives when the public self intersects with the deeply personal self. Further, there is little question that my movement to faith came about because of something that I could only call grace, which allowed me to discern in Christianity a series of beliefs and tenets that transcended (a word, by the way, that I use sparingly and with great caution), and at the same time, that managed to accommodate the peculiarities of my distinctive existence, my discourse, my politics, my history, my fears, my anxieties, my education, and my sense of culture. At the heart of this transformation, this conversion, if you will, was a way of viewing faith that would later find language in a line by T.S. Eliot that I only really started to understand as relevant to more than art in 1994, as I finished the last touches of my epic poem, *Prophets*, which, arguably, could be read as the first serious effort to address my faith in the copious manner that I felt was needed at that point: "For us, there is only the trying, the rest is not our business" ("East Coker").

"Great Is Thy Faithfulness" does not, I can say, have the kind of impact on my sense of the world that, say, Bob Marley's "Give Thanks and Praises" has whenever I hear it. But I would never say that one is more important to me than the other. "Give Thanks and Praises" roots itself in the spirit of thanksgiving, of gratitude, and of appreciation:

> If Jah didn't love I
> If I didn't love I,
> Would I be around today,
> Would I be around to say,
> Give thanks and praises,
> Give thanks and praises?

And because Marley offers this song in a music that I feel owns me as much as I can claim to own it, I am constantly affirmed by what it does to my body, my mind, and my spirit. Yet, when I sing the final verse of "Great Is Thy

Faithfulness," I do find rolling through my mind a litany of the reasons for gratitude—some even deeply secretive—that I carry within me every day, and so I can weep as I sing this verse:

> Pardon for sin and a peace that endureth,
> thine own dear presence to cheer and to guide;
> strength for today and bright hope for tomorrow,
> blessings all mine, with ten thousand beside!

I could easily have started this reflection with the statement "I do not have a favorite hymn." This would be true. But as I think of hymns that have meaning and value to me, I find that I am drawn to this great hymn. As it happens, the limited history that I have about this song does not explain why I would choose it as a favorite hymn. The author, Thomas Obadiah Chisolm, was a rural southerner from Kentucky who lived through the period of Reconstruction and the difficult years that followed, into Jim Crow America. He wrote this song in 1923 when he was in his mid-fifties. It became popular immediately. Curiously, the language and style of the song are archaic and very 19th-century, even though he wrote it well into the 20th-century. But what he actually wrote was a poem—one of the many he wrote during his lifetime. He certainly was not a modernist poet. William Runyan, a New Yorker who grew up and lived in Kansas, set the poem to music, and these two Methodists would produce a song that they have become best known for. I have, given the sketchy history I have at this point of these two men, decided against going any deeper. I fear discovering things that would make it harder for me to focus almost exclusively on the song in the manner that suspends the intellect and elevates the emotive. In other words, I don't want to spoil the song for me. I would be hard-pressed to describe this song and lyric as an example of great literary or musical achievement. While I am not qualified to make such a pronouncement on the musical achievement, I can say that as a poem, I would describe this as at best competent and occasionally hackneyed. But it makes a case beautifully, in the way that the best sermons and speeches can make wonderful and moving cases.

There is an art to this. What I can say is that, at the end of the day, the song manages to remain important to me because I have come to associate it with key moments of my life, and during those moments, the song has had a clarity and meaningfulness for which I remain deeply grateful.

Breathe on Me, Breath of God

Breathe on me, Breath of God,
fill me with life anew,
that I may love the way you love,
and do what you would do.

Breathe on me, Breath of God,
until my heart is pure,
until my will is one with yours,
to do and to endure.

Breathe on me, Breath of God,
so shall I never die,
but live with you the perfect life
for all eternity.

Edwin Hatch 1835–1889

MARGARET GIBSON

BREATHE ON ME, BREATH OF GOD

"Breathe on me, Breath of God" comprises the first line in each of the four quatrains of this hymn. "So shall I never die," says the final stanza. Singing these words at the memorial service for my dearest friend Ellen, I felt them like a body blow, so fresh was my sense of loss. Yet even then I felt the words of the final stanza point less to the theoretical endless time of an afterlife, more to a realization of eternity while alive—the expanded present moment, the eternal Now in which one experiences essential Being, or the presence of God.

Really singing a hymn, alone or with others, can at times be like chanting in Buddhist practice prior to sitting meditation. Singing or chanting, the mind clears of self-consciousness and trivia as deeper breath takes us more into the body, where presence mysteriously is. Really singing or chanting, one may experience, as in meditation, a shift in consciousness: one is no longer breathed *on*; one is being breathed. Both singing and chanting are first steps toward "practicing eternity," which in the *Tao Te Ching* means "returning to the Source."

But you have to really sing the hymn! No self-consciousness about the person in the next pew hearing your less than perfect voice, alas.

The first stanza sets the petitioner's intention: Breathe on me, *that I may love*, letting love inform what one does, what one endures. And then the hymn outlines a three-fold path. That I may love, breathe on me; and the practice of the breath leads to purity of heart, unity of will, wholeness—essentially to a shift in self-knowing. One is returned to Being. Assuming that these transformations can be realized, the hymn concludes: "So shall I never die." I read "so" as "just so," not as "so that." Breathing, loving, willing one will, being whole are the ways one practices eternity while fully alive.

In each stanza, sounding E-sharp in the second line highlights key phrases ("life anew," "is pure," "wholly thine," "never die.") The melancholy shift in pitch confirms that it is from an awareness of incompleteness that longing and the path to awakened love begin. It takes courage to sing; it takes courage to live—courage my friend, Ellen, manifested as her life deepened and unfolded in love, renewing itself moment by moment, breath by breath.

Tantum Ergo

Tantum ergo Sacramentum
Veneremur cernui:
Et antiquum documentum
Novo cedat ritui:
Praestet fides supplementum
Sensuum defectui,

Genitori, Genitoque
Laus et jubilatio,
Salus, honor, virtus quoque
Sit et benedictio:
Procedenti ab utroque
Compar sit laudatio.

Thomas Aquinas 1225–1274

DANA GIOIA

BABEL WAS MY HOMETOWN: SINGING THE "TANTUM ERGO" IN '60S L.A.

When I was a child in parochial school, we began each morning with daily Mass. My mother worked nights, and no one in my family was an early riser. I inevitably arrived late to church. The nuns stared disapprovingly as I slipped in among my more punctual classmates in our assigned pews. This daily dose of shame was good training for later life. It made me immune to peer pressure.

The Mass, which was conducted entirely in Latin, meant little to me. I endured it respectfully as a mandatory exercise. I was relieved when the service ended, and we filed off to our classrooms across the street. What impressed me was the church itself. St. Joseph's was larger than the old Los Angeles cathedral. It was one of only two buildings in my hometown of Hawthorne, California that might have been called beautiful. (The other was the Plaza, an old movie palace—now torn down.) I liked being inside St. Joseph's lofty, cool interior, which was illuminated by tall stained glass windows depicting the saints and apostles.

On the first Friday of each month, however, there was another ceremony called the Benediction. Having already attended Mass in the morning, we were marched into church again in the afternoon to participate in a short but elaborate ritual in honor of the Eucharist.

The priest, wearing a special mantle over his robes, entered accompanied by several altar boys. Candles were lit, and great suffocating clouds of incense dispersed. As the priest approached the altar, we sang a Latin hymn called "O Salutaris Hostia." We read the verses from little laminated cards. I didn't know what the words meant. (I assumed *hostia* meant the communion host, which, of course, it didn't.) I liked singing the hymn, but it wasn't my favorite.

American Catholics have a different sense of sacred music from Protestants. Singing is less central to our traditions of worship. The gap was especially wide before the Second Vatican Council. Catholics then rarely sang in church. There was no music at ordinary Mass, even on Sundays. Music was reserved for high Mass on special feast days, and then the singing was mostly Latin chant. In my Los Angeles parish, 1960 didn't sound much different from 1660.

At Benediction, however, hymns played a central role. The music endowed the service with a sense of special occasion. Hearing St. Joseph's mighty organ fill the capacious church gave me a physical thrill. It was the most powerful live music I had ever heard. Add to that titanic rumbling the voices of 700 parochial school kids singing in Latin, led by a dozen Sisters of Providence, and you will divine my wonderment and awe.

As the priest opened the shining tabernacle at the center of the marble altar and placed the consecrated host in a golden monstrance, we stood to sing a short hymn in veneration of the Eucharist. This hymn, the "Tantum Ergo," has haunted me for the past sixty years. At each service I waited for it to begin, then sang in a blissful trance. It always ended too soon.

If you don't know what the words mean, don't worry; neither did I. Nor do I intend to translate them now. That is the point of the essay.

By third grade, I had the text indelibly memorized, though the only word I understood was *sacramentum*. The literal meaning of the words seemed unimportant compared to the experience of singing. Back then I felt no genuine attachment to what the sisters reverently referred to as "the Blessed Sacrament." (That devotion came much later.) The Eucharist was mostly an abstract idea. I sensed a sanctity in which I could not participate. But as I stood singing this short hymn with all my friends and teachers, I physically felt enraptured and exhilarated in the act of veneration.

As an adult, I can't accurately judge whether that experience was spiritual or aesthetic. I suspect that those two categories of perception are more interdependent than most people believe, especially in a child. I do know from my earliest memories that "Tantum Ergo" struck me as penetratingly sublime. Those two minutes of each month were more beautiful than anything outside the church doors on the ugly streets of my hometown. The hymn acquired private meaning—a web of deep longings and associations, of intellectual and spiritual awakenings that I didn't yet understand.

I rarely received communion, usually just at Christmas and Easter. We had been instructed only to receive the sacrament in "the state of grace." In my convoluted young mind, I was a notorious sinner. Even before puberty, I always felt guilty about something.

Being different from other kids—dreamy, solitary, bookish—my mere existence felt vaguely culpable. Unless I dashed directly from the confessional to the communion rail, I would stumble back into perdition. So it wasn't the Mass, which I attended listlessly six times a week, that brought me into the mysteries of faith; it was the infrequent Benedictions. Only there I momentarily lost my self-consciousness in joyful musical communion—singing ancient and enigmatic words in honor of an inexplicable transubstantiation.

In college I discovered that the intricately rhymed verses had been written by St. Thomas Aquinas for the new feast of Corpus Christi the year before Dante was born. The poem, therefore, dates to a specific moment in Western culture. It appeared just as Latin was about to give way to Italian as a literary language, and the Middle Ages were moving toward the Renaissance. That fact now seems significant to me.

Babel was my hometown. I was raised in 13th-century L.A. in a Spanish-speaking neighborhood by Italian immigrants and assimilated mestizos who worshipped in Latin in a city whose official language was English. Latin was not a dead language, it was simply the one reserved for sacred things—like singing—in a place full of competing dialects. Even as a child, I watched my family's parlance change, as English superseded the languages of the older generation. No, the "Tantum Ergo" didn't feel foreign. Old words brought over from an old world were my daily reality.

The old practices, as Aquinas noted, give way to new rites ("Et antiquum documentum / Novo cedat ritui."). By the time I finished high school, Vatican II had dropped Latin from the Mass and most rituals. We still prayed in Latin but now only in Latin class when we stood to recite a quick "Pater Noster" before digging into another forty lines of Virgil. At Mass we now sang folksy anthems composed by amateur Jesuit musicians. If Hell has a hymnal, these tunes will fill its opening pages. Hardly anyone sang. The crowd at Sunday Mass grew smaller every year.

No one recognized the banality of the new liturgy as keenly as a California teenager. For me, *aggiornamento* became *addio*. After graduating from high school in 1969, I stopped going to Mass for nearly twenty years, except on Christmas and Easter with my mother. I never left the Church. I just stopped showing up. The hunger remained, unsatisfied. Finally in middle age, I accepted the bad music as punishment for my sins and rejoined as a communicant.

Over the years I have learned that I was not the only kid deeply affected by the hymn. When the "Tantum Ergo" is mentioned to Catholics of my generation, often as not, somebody starts singing. I have watched that happen, even in bars. The words and tune arouse deep communal memories.

Aquinas's hymn even ended up in my libretto for the opera "Tony Caruso's Final Broadcast." When I suggested employing the "Tantum Ergo" to the composer Paul Salerni, he immediately began singing the words over the phone. We ended up using the melody twice in the opera—once with the traditional words and tune, then later with the melody inverted to create a new chorale. A few years later over lunch at the USC faculty club, I mentioned the hymn to the historian Kevin Starr. After singing the first stanza, he provided a theological exposition in his booming voice. "'Praetest fides supplementum,' Dana! 'Faith provides a supplement for the defects of our senses!'" Conversation stopped at nearby tables. Yes, the hymn has an alarming effect on old Catholics.

My particular affection for the hymn probably originates in a combination of personal and impersonal factors. First, there was the resonant beauty of Aquinas' verse set to the stately 18th-century tune by Samuel Webbe. Second, there was my personal experience of singing the words repeatedly for years with my friends in the first grand space I had ever seen. Finally, there was the mystery of the Eucharist, which I first understood not from theological instruction but through the beauty of song.

As an artist, the Latin hymns taught me something else—that art is mysterious. It reaches us in ways we don't fully understand. The literal sense of a song or a poem is only part of its meaning. Physical sound and rhythm exercise a power of enchantment that eludes paraphrase. Our intuition often outpaces our intellect, and music anticipates meaning. He who sings prays twice, sometimes unaware.

Immortal, Invisible, God Only Wise

Immortal, invisible, God only wise,
in light inaccessible hid from our eyes,
most blessed, most glorious, the Ancient of Days,
almighty, victorious, Thy great name we praise.

Unresting, unhasting, and silent as light,
nor wanting, nor wasting, thou rulest in might;
Thy justice, like mountains, high soaring above,
Thy clouds, which are fountains of goodness and love.

To all life thou givest, to both great and small,
in all life thou livest, the true life of all;
we blossom and flourish as leaves on the tree,
and wither and perish, but naught changeth Thee.

Great Father of glory, pure Father of light,
thine angels adore Thee, all veiling their sight;
all praise we would render, O help us to see
'tis only the splendor of light hideth Thee!

Walter Chalmers Smith 1824–1908

LORNA GOODISON

"IMMORTAL, INVISIBLE, GOD ONLY WISE"

As a child, growing up on the island of Jamaica, it seemed to me that people, especially women, were always singing hymns as they went about their business. Women bending low over wash tubs, or standing knee deep in swift running rivers, would produce scrub rhythms from the friction of soaped cloth rubbed hard between fists; and over that wash–wash rhythm, they would moan hymns like "What a Friend We Have in Jesus."

Women ironing would sing too, accompanying their hymns with the thump and slide of heavy clothes irons. One especially weighty iron was known as a "self-heater" because it had a hollow interior designed to hold hell-hot coals. Perhaps I imagined this, but the washerwomen seemed to favor hymns about sins being washed white as snow—something most Jamaicans had never witnessed first-hand—and the ironing women seemed to like hymns that lamented our trespasses and sins and the consequent fear of hell. I like to think that the Island was girdled round by a kind of eremitical domestic holiness when those women sang.

On the streets of Kingston, preachers, often from Revivalist or Pocomania groups formed from the syncretization of African and European religions, would rock out spirited versions of Christian hymns that married—as one of our philosophers, Rex Nettleford, said—the melodies of Europe with the rhythms of Africa. Salvation Army brass bands with their booming kettle drums contributed stirring renditions of hymns as they marched out from the Bramwell Booth Memorial Hall out onto the streets of the city, there to lift up the fallen and convert the wayward.

Hymns were sung at political gatherings. "There Were Ninety and Nine" was raised at every meeting of the People's National Party, because it was the favorite hymn of Norman Washington Manley, often called the father of modern Jamaica. Jamaicans call this hymn and others like it "Sankeys" after the powerful revival style hymns performed by the great American Evangelist and baritone Ira D. Sankey.

Christian hymns were also routinely repurposed by Rastafarians, a religious sect who regard their main mission as the decolonization of the minds of African–Jamaicans; so a sankey like "If You Only Knew the Blessing That Salvation Brings," sung at a Rastafarian gathering or "reasoning," would become "If You Only Knew the Blessing Rastafari Brings." Performed in a hypnotic chanting style and underscored by powerful explosive drumming, such hymns became anthems of resistance, especially when delivered in the thunderous basso profundo of the great Rastafarian elder Mortimo Planno, who was Bob Marley's spiritual advisor.

But my mother and her people were Anglicans—or, as she preferred to say, they belonged to the Church of England. Her father, in addition to being a village lawyer, was the catechist in the local Anglican church, and so my mother and her people all grew up entirely comfortable with the language of the Book of Common Prayer and very familiar with hymns written by some of the finest poets in the English Language.

And my mother relied on hymns to get her through the daily rounds and numerous common tasks involved in raising nine children on not a lot of money. She would sing these hymns in a funny out of breath style, opting to hum some lines low under her breath as if internalizing their deeper meaning, and singing others out loud, offering them up for all to hear in bursts of lament, praise, petition, or thanksgiving. Ironically, one of her favorite hymns, "Immortal, Invisible, God Only Wise," was written in 1867 not by an Anglican but by a Scottish Methodist minister, Reverend W. Chalmers Smith, and it has become my favorite hymn.

"Immortal, Invisible, God Only Wise" is a hymn I love and admire mainly because it is a triumph of a praise song that uses words to describe the indescribable; something to which any hard-grafting poet can relate. It does so in what in the English moral philosopher Mary Warnock calls "beautiful unordinary language," the only language fitting to describe God who cannot be seen through mortal eyes; who is immortal, most wise, most blessed, and most glorious; and above all, most worthy of the ultimate honorific: "The Ancient of

Days," who is almighty and victorious and whose great name we praise.

When I was an art student I always used to pause as I would sing that opening verse and picture William Blake's fiery rendering of Urizen setting a compass to the earth; but some time ago something in me shifted, and now when I sing that line I see instead my mother, her hair gone completely white, contained in that bright circle of Blake's making, and she is measuring yards of richly brocaded fabric with her worn dressmaking tape measure.

I love, just love, what happens in the second verse of this hymn, how one of the loveliest surprises I know of in all of writing occurs. The Immortal Invisible, who does not rest or make haste, is described as "Silent as LIGHT." Not night, but light. Lovely silent light which is invoked in every verse except the third. And then the old adage "Waste not, want not" becomes a divine attribute of a mighty God, who does not waste nor want. All throughout this hymn, there are graceful gestures connecting the Divine to the daily in lovely numinous hints.

I have sung this hymn at least one hundred times at morning assembly during the years I attended St. Hugh's School for girls founded for the education of young ladies by the Anglican church in Kingston over one hundred years ago. I have sung it in churches in Ann Arbor, Michigan and in Toronto and Vancouver, and at least once in Durham Cathedral in England. My husband, Ted Chamberlin, and I chose it as the hymn for our wedding, so it has a very special place in my worship life, but these days it seems to have taken on even greater significance as I watch the news and I find myself turning to the lines "Thy justice like mountains high soaring above, / Thy clouds which are fountains of goodness and love." These words reassure me that no matter how much injustice there is in the world, there is an ultimate source of justice, one that can only be measured by the heights of mountains. I am reassured, too, that there is a supply of goodness and love, which comes down from the clouds like rain, or snow, and because this hymn is powered by the unordinary, this cloud-source of goodness and love paradoxically flows like a fountain.

I feel the need to remind myself of the constant nature of the divine that "nought changeth" these days as I watch the news. Even as we mortals blossom and flourish as leaves on a tree . . . and then, without a doubt, wither and perish.

In the original version of this hymn, the penultimate verse contains these lines, which were changed (by the Wesleys?): "But of all Thy rich graces, this grace Lord impart, / take the veil from our faces the vile from our hearts." I wish they had kept those words; for the graceful turn of veil into vile—a hard, but so honest word which resonates with those of us who are painfully aware that we often are, as the Book of Common prayer says, "most miserable offenders."

But mostly this is my favorite hymn because it almost succeeds in describing what no one can ever fully describe: the greatest of all mysteries that is veiled in silent light.

Silent Night

Silent night, holy night!
All is calm, all is bright.
Round yon virgin mother and child!
Holy Infant so tender and mild,
sleep in heavenly peace,
sleep in heavenly peace.

Silent night, holy night!
Shepherds quake at the sight;
glories stream from heaven afar,
heavenly hosts sing "Alleluia!
Christ the Savior is born!
Christ the Savior is born!"

Silent night, holy night!
Son of God, love's pure light.
Radiant beams from Thy holy face,
with the dawn of redeeming grace.
Jesus, Lord, at your birth,
Jesus, Lord, at your birth.

Joseph Mohr 1792–1849

JASON GRAY

"SILENT NIGHT"

What do you do when your organ is broken? In Obendorf, Austria, newly split from its sister city across the Salzach in Bavaria, it's 1818 and the Napoleonic Wars have left their mark. It's cold and damp and Christmas is approaching. Father Joseph Mohr is the new priest at St. Nikolaus and requests that Franz Gruber (no relation to Hans) write a melody for the poem he'd written two years earlier. Gruber is the schoolmaster and the organist, but there is no organ. Silent pipes. Gruber plays the only instrument at hand, the guitar.

Arguably the most well-known Christmas carol ever was written out of necessity.

At least that's how the story was told to me by another member of Central Presbyterian Church, an adult I was playing guitar with in the church's contemporary music ensemble—two guitarists, a bass player, and the organist moving over to a Casio. I was getting very involved with the church at this point in my life, in high school. I was active with the youth group, joined the choir, and was showing off my new guitar skills in our nascent contemporary music group. We weren't megachurch-ready, but we had a certain charm. My faith was growing, to be sure, but I was also in love with pretty much every female member of the youth group in some way or another. I was sure I'd marry one of them (I did not). This is probably why church has never seemed so enthralling as it once was, but I think almost everything is that way—nothing *seems* to matter as much as it did in high school. I recognize this is not a great reflection on my faith.

The story's reason for the problematic organ varies, from mice chewing on wires to rusty pipes to simply choosing a well-made guitar over a low-quality organ.

The guitar is portable, but doesn't have the largest range. It is quiet and no match for the organ's volume. But if you want space in between your soundwaves, if you want each note to have its own life, it will give it to you.

Although, you rarely hear the song performed in its original arrangement.

Bing Crosby's recording of "Silent Night" (full orchestra and choir) is the third-bestselling single of all time, with around 30 million copies sold. (His version of "White Christmas" is first on that list—need we any more proof that we are a secular people, despite our many protests?). That album of Crosby's, *Merry Christmas*, with just a headshot of him wearing a Santa hat and a holly bowtie—my family wore that out on Christmas mornings. And I continued to do so as a grown up, from magnetic tape to lasered plastic to digital files, always around the time the toilet paper from Mischief Night began to disintegrate from the trees.

I whistle and hum carols pretty regularly throughout the year (most likely "Winter Wonderland" or "Rudolf.") This surprises most everyone I come in contact with, but I'm not sure why. Yes, it's out of season, but they are imminently hummable tunes, and how many of us in the Western world grew up hearing them more than any other class of song? "Silent Night" is not one I whistle though. It is one of the more somber tunes of the season—but not the most somber—I have to give that to "In the Bleak Midwinter."

"Silent Night" is Joseph Mohr's only hymn translated into English, and it is Gruber's only still-known melody, though he reportedly wrote over a hundred. The Presbyterian hymnal includes four verses, but the fourth is an anomaly—it does not correspond to the original German text or the J. Freeman Young translation.

Americans sing the song out of order. Also incompletely. The original German hymn is six verses, but most of us know only three—the first, the sixth, then the second. Which seems like a good metaphor for me as a Christian, incomplete and out of order (perhaps all of us, but I won't speak for everyone).

In the English version, with its missing verses, we don't sing about the salvation and mercy brought to us, the capital-F fatherly love, the fact that it was all planned from the beginning. The original German text narrates the story in the three lines between the refrains that bookend each stanza. We focus on the couple, mother and child, and the shepherds, and then again the baby—the people in the story. Whether intentional or not on the part of J.

Freeman Young, the translator, I think there's a good idea there. The intangible, though wonderful, things we hope are part of this story are stripped away, leaving us with what we actually know is there. The people. I don't mean to be sacrilegious; only to suggest that the winnowing down to the human elements perhaps contributes to the carol's importance to a great deal of the world.

At midnights throughout the Christian world the tune rings on as lights go down and candles bloom to life. My favorite moment in all of liturgy is that moment the organ stops in the song and leaves only the congregation's voices singing. For one moment, at least, the world around you is still. Consider all that would follow from that one night in Bethlehem. A man who would inspire a dozen, then dozens, hundreds, thousands, millions, to turn the other cheek, to build houses for the destitute, to stop a battle for one day, to love one another and die, but also to force others to accept him, to kill for his rejection. This is the mixed blessing of Christmas, or perhaps the mixed inheritance—the blessing may have been pure, but not always its interpretation.

Franz Gruber made the best out of what he was given. I don't know if I can say that about myself, or how many of us can. But it is what I think about when I hear "Silent Night." When your organ is broken, find another way of making music.

O Come, O Come, Emmanuel

O come, O come, Emmanuel,
and ransom captive Israel
that mourns in lonely exile here
until the Son of God appear.

Refrain:
Rejoice! Rejoice! Emmanuel
shall come to you, O Israel.

O come, O Wisdom from on high,
who ordered all things mightily;
to us the path of knowledge show
and teach us in its ways to go.

O come, O come, great Lord of might,
who to your tribes on Sinai's height
in ancient times did give the law
in cloud and majesty and awe.

O come, O Branch of Jesse's stem,
unto your own and rescue them!
From depths of hell your people save,
and give them victory o'er the grave.

O come, O Key of David, come
and open wide our heavenly home.
Make safe for us the heavenward road
and bar the way to death's abode.

O come, O bright and morning star,

and bring us comfort from afar!
Dispel the shadows of the night
and turn our darkness into light.

O come, O king of nations, bind
in one the hearts of all mankind.
Bid all our sad divisions cease
and be yourself our king of peace.

Translated by John Mason Neale (1818–1866)

LINDA GREGERSON

"O COME, O COME, EMMANUEL"

I loved them all, the hymns we sang in our red brick Methodist church on Christmas Eve. There was always snow, it never failed us, the streetlamps cast lovely pools of light and shadow on the shoveled walks. We called it midnight service, though it actually began an hour earlier; we would have eaten our dinner and opened our presents. The men in our family stayed home. I loved all the Christmas hymns, but one of them was magic.

I understand now—I've learned it on the internet—that it was another of those marvelous Victorians (*The Oxford English Dictionary*! *The Dictionary of National Biography* ! Where would we be without them?) to whom we owe the English verses. In its original Latin, "Veni Veni Emmanuel" was a product of the medieval monastery, dating back to the 12th century at the very latest. John Mason Neale (1818–1866) discovered the verses in the appendix of an 18th-century manuscript and published them, in English, in his *Mediaeval Hymns and Sequences* (1851). Three years later, in *The Hymnal Noted*, Thomas Helmore paired them with a melody he claimed to have found in "a French Missal in the National Library, Lisbon." That missal has never been relocated, but in 1966 the musicologist (and Augustinian canoness) Mary Berry discovered the same melody in a 15th-century manuscript in the Bibliothèque Nationale. The English hymn celebrates a longed-for birth, so I find it rather poignant to learn that this tune, at least in its 15th-century incarnation, served as a processional chant for burials.

But then, the hymn I love has always been a mixture of celebration and mourning:

> O come, O come, Emmanuel,
> And ransom captive Israel,
> That mourns in lonely exile here
> Until the Son of God appear.

Rejoice! Rejoice! Emmanuel
Shall come to you, O Israel.

As witness to its mingled joy and sorrow, the hymn is set in a minor key.

I knew nothing of its history, of course, when I sang this hymn with all the good people who filled the pews of the Cary Methodist Church on Christmas Eve. I doubt I knew what Emmanuel meant and I didn't think to wonder. I only knew—I took it in somehow with the very first chords of the organ prelude— that we were welcoming a mystery. Number 211 in the Methodist Hymnal, key of E minor: E is where the hymn comes "home," and minor keys are good for mystery. In the Book of Isaiah, the prophesied Messiah is called Emmanuel. In the Book of Matthew, an angel tells Joseph that his betrothed is the virgin of the prophecy, her child the child of God. Emmanuel, as the Evangelist is careful to specify, means God-with-us. There is sweetness in the minor chord: discovering what he had taken to be her shame, Joseph had planned to put Mary aside "privily." Joseph is a just man.

Above the altar in our red brick church was a single stained glass window, very small, circular, depicting the Holy Ghost in the form of a bird. Our one gesture toward ostentation. In the heat of the English Reformation, the Puritan Richard Baxter used to rail against the "painted obscure sermons" of the Anglican preachers, pronouncing them to be no better than "the Painted Glass in the Windows that keep out the Light." I had never heard of Richard Baxter when I lived in Cary, Illinois; I'd barely heard of the Reformation. No one had ever preached to me about the dangers of idolatry. But the stained glass windows in the Roman Catholic Church on the other side of town, like the bleak dormitories for the nuns, struck me as slightly sinister. The priest lived in a fine new house.

It was only by accident, really, that we were Methodists at all. Norwegian immigrants belonged to the church of Martin Luther. But when my grandparents moved from Chicago in the 1920s, our small town had only one Protestant Church on offer, and it was the church of John Wesley. My grandfather was a fine craftsman, meticulous in his pin-striped overalls. It was he who, on a windless day, climbed the steeple to apply gold leafing to the cross. Modest ostentation: a plain gold cross on a plain white steeple, upright in praise, and the overalls freshly ironed, women did that then. The windows in the nave were tall and broad, with panes of transparent glass.

So it's ironic, really—it quite betrays me—to realize that I must have loved this hymn for its whiff of the monastery: chalice and incense smuggled in by way of the minor chord. There's a moment, a breathtaking moment, when the meter defies expectation. Everything has been steady-as-you-go, four/four time, all quarter notes and dotted halves. But during that remarkable refrain, just when you expect to dwell on the last syllable of the holy name for a count of three, as every verse before this has prepared you to do, the hymn leaps forward and anticipates itself by half a measure. No breath, no stately pause: "Emmanuel / shall come to you," as though rushing to arrival. Those missed beats never fail to stop my heart.

And they rhyme somehow with the promise and foreboding built into that second long era of expectation, the one believers inhabit now, because the child so fervently awaited has come and been killed and has promised to come again. *Two women shall be grinding at the mill; the one shall be taken, and the other left.* The minor chords of a hymn sung toward midnight in a small town blanketed by snow. *He shall come like a bridegroom, he shall come like a thief in the night.* And when we least expect it, the leap across a missing half-measure.

In a poem, or a painting, or a stage play, it's the rarest and most wonderful of all effects, to be taken by surprise, even when you know the surprise is coming. Repeatable surprise. It shouldn't be possible. It requires something more than double awareness or divided consciousness: it requires authentic inhabitation of two noncommensurate states of expectation. I suppose in this it is like faith. I don't believe in hell. I don't believe in the afterlife, except perhaps in the hearts of those who love us. But the promise of a savior in a minor key and the promise of judgment in those dark gospel verses—dark good news— never fail to seize my heart.

O Little Town of Bethlehem

O little town of Bethlehem,
how still we see thee lie!
Above thy deep and dreamless sleep
the silent stars go by.
Yet in Thy dark streets shineth
the everlasting light;
the hopes and fears of all the years
are met in thee tonight.

For Christ is born of Mary
and, gathered all above,
while mortals sleep, the angels keep
their watch of wond'ring love.
O morning stars, together
proclaim the holy birth,
and praises sing to God the King,
and peace to men on earth.

How silently, how silently
the wondrous gift is giv'n!
So God imparts to human hearts
the blessings of His heav'n.
No ear may hear His coming,
but in this world of sin,
where meek souls will receive Him still
the dear Christ enters in.

O holy Child of Bethlehem,
descend to us, we pray.
Cast out our sin and enter in;

be born in us today.
We hear the Christmas angels
the great glad tidings tell;
O come to us, abide with us,
our Lord Emmanuel.

Phillips Brooks (1835–1893)

ROBERT HASS

"O LITTLE TOWN OF BETHLEHEM"

Christmas carols seem to come from nowhere, but some of the best-known derive from the hymn tradition of Victorian America. One of them is "O Little Town of Bethlehem." It was written by Phillips Brooks (1835–1893), an Episcopal priest, born in Boston and educated at Harvard, who was rector of the Church of the Holy Trinity in Philadelphia.

An eloquent speaker, Brooks was, as an old man, invited to preach at Westminster Abbey and before Queen Victoria at Windsor. He came to public attention when he was invited to compose a prayer for the Harvard Commemoration of the Civil War Dead in 1865. A year later he wrote "O Little Town of Bethlehem" for his Sunday school. It was first performed by children in Philadelphia at Christmas in 1868.

This explains something to me about the power of the song, especially its plain and exquisite first stanza. It is a poem about Christmas and about peace written when the butchery at Shiloh and Gettysburg and Bull Run was still a wound in public memory, and it carries, in the aftermath of that war, the intensity of the yearning for peace. Poignant for us, because Bethlehem continues, in our time, to be a focus of that longing.

The hymn is written in the common meter—alternating eight and six syllable lines, the same measure Emily Dickinson used, with the shorter second and fourth lines rhyming. It's interesting to read the hymn as a poem—in the tradition that produced "Rock of Ages" and "Amazing Grace" and "Shall We Gather at the River"—when you know its historical context. "Wondering love" is another striking phrase. We must give the angels a lot to wonder about.

Caedmon's Hymn

Nu sculon herigean   heofonrices Weard
Meotodes meahte   and his modgeþanc,
weorc Wuldor-Fæder,   swa he wundra gehwæs
ece Drihten   or onstealde
He ærest sceop   ielda bearnum
Heofon to hrofe   halig Scyppend
ða middangeard   moncynnes Weard,
ece Drihten   æfter teode
firum foldan   Frea ælmihtig

Caedmon, composed sometime between 658–680

EDWARD HIRSCH

CAEDMON'S HYMN

English poetry began with a vision. It started with the holy trance of a 7th-century figure called Caedmon, an illiterate herdsman, who now stands at the top of the English literary tradition as the initial Anglo-Saxon or Old English poet of record, the first to compose Christian poetry in his own language.

The story goes that Caedmon, who was employed by the monastery of Whitby, invariably fled when it was his turn to sing during a merry social feast. He was ashamed he had never had any songs to contribute. But one night a voice came to Caedmon in a dream and asked him to sing a song. When Caedmon responded that he had no idea how to sing, the voice commanded him to sing about the source of all created things ("Sing to me the beginning of all things"). "Thereupon," as the monk known as the Venerable Bede tells it in his *Ecclesiastical History of the English People* (731), "Caedmon began to sing verses which he had never heard before in praise of God the creator."

Bede embedded a Latin translation of the Anglo-Saxon poem in his history. He probably translated it into Latin in order to make the poem available to an international audience of clerics, but it's also possible that he was translating it from Latin. No one knows the priority of these texts—in manuscripts, the English version survives alongside Latin translations. Here is a West Saxon rendition of the inspired poem called "Caedmon's Hymn," which was composed between 658 and 680.

> Now we must praise   the Protector of the heavenly kingdom
> the might of the Measurer   and His mind's purpose,
> the work of the Father of Glory,   as He for each of his wonders,
> the eternal Lord,   established a beginning.
> He shaped first   for the sons of the Earth
> heaven as a roof,   the Holy Maker;
> then the Middle-World,   mankind's Guardian,

the eternal Lord,   made afterwards,
solid ground for men,   the almighty Lord.

Caedmon's dream was a sign he had become a poet. It was a signal of poetic vocation. A clumsy unschooled peasant is suddenly gifted with the power of song. It is also possible, as later scholars have speculated, that Caedmon was actually trained as a Germanic bard or scop, but concealed his knowledge of pagan poetry from the monks, who would have disapproved of what Bede calls "vain and idle songs." Caedmon took an oral form that was used to venerate royalty and refashioned it to praise the Lord, God the monarch. His hymn, his only surviving composition, is a praise poem to the Almighty, like the Latin canticle "Benedicte, omnia opera domini," which embraces all of creation ("O all ye Works of the Lord, bless ye the Lord: Praise Him, and magnify Him for ever."). It encapsulates the basic form of Old English or Germanic poetry: two half-lines, each containing two stressed and two or more unstressed syllables.

Another way of describing this is as one four-stress line with a medial caesura. It stacks two or three alliterations per line and piles up the epithets for God, who is Guardian ("Weard"), Measurer ("Meotod"), Glory-Father ("Wuldor-Fæder"), eternal Lord ("ece Drihten"), Creator or Holy Maker ("Scyppend"), and almighty Master ("Frea ælmihtig"). What came to Caedmon in a dream was not just a story, which he would have known already, but also a new prosody.

Caedmon connects the energy of language with the power of divine spirit, and his religious poetry of praise inaugurates a tradition. It's possible, too, that Bede was promoting that tradition via Caedmon. This way of connecting language to the divine looks backward to Genesis 1 and forward to Thomas Traherne, Henry Vaughan, and Christopher Smart, who sings of the transcendent virtue of praise itself. Here, for example, is stanza fifty of Smart's 18th-century poem of benediction, "A Song to David":

PRAISE above all—for praise prevails;
Heap up the measure, load the scales,

And good to goodness add:
The gen'rous soul her Savior aids,
But peevish obloquy degrades;
The Lord is great and glad.

Caedmon's impulsive song looks forward to William Blake, Gerard Manley Hopkins, and even Walt Whitman, who embraces and challenges us to embrace all the works of creation: "Divine I am inside and out, and I make holy whatever I touch or am touched from" ("Song of Myself"). It stands behind W. H. Auden's radiant and intricate sonnet of instruction, "Anthem," which begins: "Let us praise our Maker, with true passion extol Him." And it inspired Denise Levertov's poem "Caedmon," which concludes with the vision of a clumsy untutored clodhopper suddenly flaming with inspiration: "nothing was burning," Caedmon cries out, "nothing but I, as that hand of fire / touched my lips and scorched my tongue / and pulled my voice / into the ring of the dance."

"Now we must praise," Caedmon instructs us, and thus touches upon one of the primary and permanent impulses in poetry—a calling to more life, a form of blessing, a way of cherishing a world that shines out with radiant particularity.

Onward, Christian Soldiers

Onward, Christian soldiers,
marching as to war,
with the cross of Jesus
going on before!
Christ, the royal Master,
leads against the foe;
forward into battle,
see his banner go!

Refrain:
Onward, Christian soldiers,
marching as to war,
with the cross of Jesus
going on before!

At the sign of triumph
Satan's host doth flee;
on, then, Christian soldiers,
on to victory!
Hell's foundations quiver
at the shout of praise;
brothers, lift your voices,
loud your anthems raise!

Like a mighty army
moves the church of God;
brothers, we are treading
where the saints have trod;
we are not divided;
all one body we,

one in hope and doctrine,
one in charity.

Onward, then, ye people,
join our happy throng;
blend with ours your voices
in the triumph song:
Glory, laud, and honor,
unto Christ the King;
this thro' countless ages
men and angels sing.

Sabine Baring-Gould (1834–1924)

JAY HOPLER

"ONWARD, CHRISTIAN SOLDIERS"

1.

Sabine Baring-Gould's *The Book of Werewolves: Being an Account of a Terrible Superstition* was published in 1865 and remains the definitive work on lycanthropy. That same year, Baring-Gould penned "Onward, Christian Soldiers," one of the English-speaking world's most problematic hymns. Like the werewolf, a man who is also a beast, "Onward, Christian Soldiers" is, at once, what it is and what it isn't, at least what it shouldn't be: a hymn with its roots firmly grounded in scripture (2 Timothy 2:3-4, Matthew 10:34, Luke 22:36) and a martial anthem that is antithetical to the idea of Christianity as a peaceful religion. The dissonance created by its simultaneous occupation of those two diametrically opposed spaces makes it seem forever out of tune.

2.

As far as Baring-Gould was concerned, "Onward, Christian Soldiers" was neither a martial anthem, nor a hymn, at least not a hymn he imagined would ever appear in an adult hymnal. Originally entitled "Hymn for Procession with Cross and Banners" it was written as a children's processional. Baring-Gould is quoted in the October 19, 1895 issue of *The Churchman*:

> It was written in a very simple fashion, without a thought of publication. Whit-Monday is a great day for school festivals in Yorkshire, and one Whit-Monday it was arranged that our school should join forces with that of a neighboring village. I wanted the children to sing when marching from one village to the other, but couldn't think of anything

quite suitable, so I sat up at night resolved to write something myself. "Onward, Christian Soldiers" was the result.

In 1865, Baring-Gould was the curate of Horbury Bridge, and those "Christian soldiers" he was urging on were his young charges. And they weren't "marching as to war," they were walking from Horbury Bridge to St. Peter's Church in celebration of the Pentecost.

3.

For out of Zion shall go forth the law,/and the word of the Lord from Jerusalem./ He shall judge between the nations, and shall decide for many peoples;/and they shall beat their swords into plowshares,/and their spears into pruning hooks;/nation shall not lift up sword against nation,/neither shall they learn war anymore.

4.

Isaiah's got a good beat, but you can't march to it.

5.

The best thing you can say about "Onward Christian Soldiers" is that the Nazis didn't appropriate its tune for their national anthem the way they did with "Glorious Things of Thee Are Spoken."

6.

But there are plenty of people who love "Onward, Christian Soldiers." An attempt by the Methodist Church to purge it from their hymnal in 1986 failed after the editors received more than 10,000 angry letters insisting they keep it. Still, the standard defense of the hymn, that its militaristic language is appropriate because Christians need to be reminded that they are locked in a perpetual battle against sin and the forces of evil, feels wrongs to me. Christians don't need to be reminded that we are locked in a battle with the forces of evil. If anything, we need to be reminded that human beings are essentially good, that the light of the Divine shines in everyone regardless of who they are or what they believe, that the evil in the world is of our own making.

7.

After all the cruel and unspeakable things that have been done in the name of "Christ, the royal Master," I worry that we wouldn't be the soldiers if He ever were to lead an army "against the foe." We'd be the foe.

There Is a Green Hill Far Away

There is a green hill far away,
without a city wall,
where the dear Lord was crucified,
who died to save us all.

We may not know, we cannot tell,
what pains he had to bear,
but we believe it was for us
he hung and suffered there.

He died that we might be forgiven,
he died to make us good,
that we might go at last to heaven,
saved by his precious blood.

There was no other good enough
to pay the price of sin;
he only could unlock the gate
of heaven, and let us in.

O dearly, dearly has he loved,
and we must love him too,
and trust in his redeeming blood,
and try his works to do.

Cecil Frances Alexander (1818–1895)

MARK JARMAN

THE GREEN HILL FAR AWAY

I do not know where I learned the Victorian poet Cecil Frances Alexander's hymn, "There Is a Green Hill Far Away." Either it was at school, Dunnikier School in Kirkcaldy, Scotland, or it was at church, St. Clair Street Church of Christ, also in Kirkcaldy, but it may have been in both places. There was no separation of church and state in Scotland, or anywhere else in the British Isles, in the 1950s, when my family lived there while my father served the church on St. Clair Street. Bible study was a weekly part of my elementary school classes, and we began and ended the school day with a hymn, and of course much of Sunday and every Wednesday night were spent at church. I also remember learning Alexander's hymns "Once in Royal David's City" and "All Things Bright and Beautiful." Along with "There Is a Green Hill Far Away," they were originally included in her collection *Hymns for Little Children.* The tune we sang it to was by William Horsley. Though there are other settings, it is Horsley's tune that has stuck in my mind. And I would not be surprised if it were Horsley's tune that has made the hymn memorable to me, but I know that is not the only reason.

There is another reason this hymn remains in my memory. Whenever I think of it, I also think of a picture that hung in the entranceway of our house on Bennochy Road, the manse, as it was called, or parsonage, where the pastor of St. Clair Street Church of Christ would live with his family. This picture was a reproduction of a massive painting by the Polish artist Jan Styka depicting the scene on Calvary, the place of the skull, Golgotha, as Christ is about to be crucified. Styka painted the picture in 1894. It is some 195 feet by 45 feet, and hangs today in Forest Lawn Memorial Gardens in Glendale, California. The reproduction that hung in the manse entryway in Kirkcaldy was very modest in size, but still large enough so that I could pick out the details. Christ stands between the two crosses already erected for the thieves and beside the cross he will be nailed to, which lies on the ground. The hill is barren and rocky and crowded with soldiers and people and at the base of the hill is Jerusalem inside its wall. The hill itself is anything but green. But in the distance, there is a line of green hills. In the scene as Styka depicted it, the hills seem very far away.

Alexander makes it clear in her hymn that Christ was crucified on a green hill, "without" or outside of "a city wall." That is where he made his sacrifice to "save us all." Not only did Alexander have a gift for setting a scene, but also for conveying basic belief with an admixture of Victorian edification. She reminds the little children to whom she is presumably speaking that no one but Jesus could be found "to pay the price of sin" because "there was no other good enough." Therefore we must not only "trust" that the blood of his sacrifice will redeem us, but must also "try his works to do." Faith without works did not amount to much in Victorian Christianity like Alexander's. And Jesus was a model of both, especially for children. In "Once in Royal David's City," Alexander's famous Christmas carol, we are reminded that Jesus grew from infancy just like us, "For he is our childhood's pattern." He was a model of obedience and good behavior.

Still, there is that imaginary green hill far away. It was probably the first emblem of pastoral that I responded to, aside from the 23rd Psalm, and it was more compelling than the imagery there, at least for me, and possibly because in Styka's painting, the green hills look like a possible escape, a place to flee. In the painting, Christ lifts his eyes, recalling Psalm 121, "I will lift up mine eyes unto the hills, from whence cometh my help." No help is coming from the green hills in the distance, but I suspect that Alexander is giving her audience an image it can picture.

She was Anglo Irish, a member of the Church of Ireland, and lived in Northern Ireland, married to an Anglican priest who would become Bishop of Derry and Archbishop of Armagh. I am sure she was perfectly capable of imagining a bare and barren hill. But she knew enough of the pastoral tradition to know that green is the color of renewal and new life, such as bestowed on the world by Christ's death and resurrection. And the memory she evokes of that hill is still green.

Her common measure quatrains are simple and theologically precise. The sense of nostalgia for a pastoral landscape begins right off the bat with "There is," for the hill though far away does still exist in what Alexander would have called the Holy Land. Then comes the transition to the historical past, the event and its purpose and its consequence for all time. Like the psalms and like folk songs, the poem includes a series of statement and reiteration, statement and enhanced restatement ("We do not know, we cannot tell," "He died that we might be forgiven, / He died to make us good," "Oh dearly, dearly has he loved, / and we must love him too . . ."). Perhaps the most interesting image occurs in stanza four: "He only could unlock the gate / of heaven, and let us in." Only Christ and no one else, even St. Peter, could take us to the wall of another city, and open the gate for us. Or we may be meant to imagine a place better than a city—a garden. It would be walled and private and yet the gardener, particularly fond of good little children, would have a key and could let us in.

My suspicion is that I am not the only child from St. Clair Street Church of Christ Sunday School or Dunnikier School in Kirkcaldy, Fife, Scotland, in the late 1950s, who remains fond of this hymn for reasons that have as much to do with personal associations as with belief. I learned to read and write there, and do sums, and became conscious of the fundamentals of Christian faith, especially from reading and singing the Psalms and the hymns of the Church. That experience has emerged in my poetry many times.

Laudes Creaturarum

Altissimu onnipotente bon signore
    tue so le laude la gloria e l' onore e onne benedictione.
Ad te solo altissimu se konfanno
    e nullu homo ene dignu te mentovare.
Laudatu si mi signore cum tucte le tue creature
    spetialmente messor lu frate sole
    lu quale iorno et allumini per loi.
E ellu è bellu e radiante cum grande splendore
    de te altissimu porta significatione.
Laudatu si mi signore per sora luna e le stelle
    in celu l' ai formate clarite e pretiose e belle.
Laudatu si mi signore per frate ventu
    e per aere e nubilo e sereno e onne tempu
    per lu quale a le tue creature dai sustentamentu.
Laudatu si mi signore per sor aqua
    la quale è multo utile e humele e pretiosa e casta.
Laudatu si mi signore per per frate focu
    per lu quale n' allumeni la nocte
    e ellu è bello e iucundo e robusto e forte.
Laudatu si mi signore per sora nostra matre terra
    la quale ne sustenta e governa
    e produce diversi fructi e coloriti fiori e erba.
Laudatu si mi signore per quilli ke perdonano per lo tue amore
    e sostengono infirmitate e tribulatione
    beati quelli ke 'l sosterranno in pace
    ke da te altissimu sirano incoronati.
Laudatu si mi signore per sora nostra morte corporale
    da la quale nullu homo vivente po skappare
    guai a quilli ke morranno in peccata mortale.
    Beati quelli ke troverà ne le tue sanctissime voluntati

ke la morte secunda no 'l poterà far male.
Laudate e benedicete lu mi signore e rengratiate
e servite a lui cum grande humilitate. Amen.

Francis of Assisi, c. 1225

Praises of the Creatures

Highest, omnipotent, good our Lord,
yours are the praises, the glory, the honor, and all blessing.
To you alone, Most High, they are owed,
and no mortal is worthy to mention you.
Be praised, my Lord, through all your creatures,
especially through my Lord Brother Sun,
who brings the day, and you shed light through him.
And he is beautiful and radiant in his grand splendor!
Of you, Most High, he bears the likeness.
Be praised, my Lord, through Sister Moon and the stars;
In heaven you formed them, bright and precious and beautiful.
Be praised, My Lord, through Brother Wind
and through the air, cloudy and serene, and through all weathers
by which you give your creatures sustenance.
Be praised, my Lord, through Sister Water,
who is so useful and humble and precious and chaste.
Be praised, my Lord, through Brother Fire,
through whom you illuminate the night;
and he is lovely and playful and robust and strong.
Be praised, my Lord, through our Sister Mother Earth,
who sustains and governs us
and who brings forth varied fruits with vibrant flowers and herbs.

Be praised, my Lord, through those who give pardon for love of you,
    and bear infirmity and tribulation;
      blessed are those who persevere in peace,
    for they will be, by you Most High, endowed a crown.
Be praised, my Lord, through our sister, Death-of-the-Flesh,
    from whom no living mortal can escape.
      Woe to those who die in mortal sin!
      Blessed whom death finds abiding in your most sacred will,
    for the second death shall do them no harm.
Praise and bless my Lord, and render thanks to Him,
    and serve Him with great humility. Amen.

Translated from the Italian by Kimberly Johnson

All Creatures of Our God and King

All creatures of our God and King,
lift up your voice and with us sing:
Alleluia, Alleluia!
O burning sun with golden beam,
and shining moon with silver gleam,
O praise Him, O praise Him,
Alleluia, alleluia, alleluia!

O rushing wind so wild and strong,
white clouds that sail in heaven along:
Alleluia, alleluia!
New rising dawn in praise rejoice;
you lights of evening find a voice,
O praise Him, O praise Him,

Alleluia, alleluia, alleluia!

Cool flowing water, pure and clear,
make music for your Lord to hear:
Alleluia, alleluia!
Fierce fire, so masterful and bright,
providing us with warmth and light,
O praise Him, O praise Him,
Alleluia, alleluia, alleluia!

Earth ever fertile, day by day
bring forth your blessings on our way:
Alleluia, alleluia!
All flowers and fruits that in you grow,
let them his glory also show,
O praise Him, O praise Him,
Alleluia, alleluia, alleluia!

All you who are of tender heart,
forgiving others, take your part:
Alleluia, alleluia!
All you who pain and sorrow bear,
praise God and on him cast your care,
O praise Him, O praise Him,
Alleluia, alleluia, alleluia!

And thou most kind and gentle death,
waiting to hush our latest breath:
Alleluia, alleluia!
Thou leadest home the child of God,
and Christ our Lord the way hath trod.
O praise Him, O praise Him,

Alleluia, alleluia, alleluia!

Let all things their Creator bless,
and worship Him in humbleness:
Alleluia, alleluia!
Praise, praise the Father, praise the Son,
and praise the Spirit, Three in One!
O praise Him, O praise Him,
Alleluia, alleluia, alleluia!

Translated from the Italian by William Henry Draper (1855–1933)

KIMBERLY JOHNSON

ON "LAUDES CREATURARUM" ("ALL CREATURES OF OUR GOD AND KING"): A POLYPHONY

In Assisi, the sky vaults clouded and serene against the foothills.

*

Pietro, known as Francesco, devoted brother of his order, put quill to 13th-century parchment and began to praise. His inspiration was the 148th Psalm, whose Hebrew exhortations spur the sun and moon, the stars and highest heavens, tempests and mountains and wingèd birds to sing their Lord's splendid name. Barchu and Hallelu.

*

In the trees that ring the great cathedral at Assisi, birds trill an antiphon in the innumerable dialects of their collected species.

*

"Laudatu si mi signore per sora nostra morte corporale," Francis wrote in his backwater dialect, "da la quale nullu homo vivente po skappare." *Be praised, my Lord, through our sister, Death-of-the-Flesh, from whom no living mortal can escape.*

*

William Henry Draper lost his first wife in childbirth. He lost his second wife in her youth. He lost three sons in World War I, and a daughter in her childhood.

*

In Francesco's hymn, the psalm's call to worship forges familial bonds, each voice enfolded into the household: *My Lord Brother Sun. Sister Moon* and *Sister Water, Brother Fire* and *Brother Wind.*

*

Twice widowed, four times unfathered, William Henry Draper served as rector of the parish church in Leeds, where, in 1919, he translated a centuries-old poem by an Umbrian monk for a Whitsunday children's concert.

*

On Whitsunday, the Assisi cathedral is afire with cloven tongues, pilgrims murmuring a babel of prayer.

*

Thou rushing wind that art so strong

*

At the wind of the day I walked the fortress wall on Assisi's hilltop as the houselights came on below. "A mighty fortress is our God," another word-dazzled monk would write three centuries after Francesco threw open the enclosures of monastic care to the lazar-house, the beggars, the birds.

*

At a piazza dinner in the hilltop town of Perugia, against which young soldier Pietro called Francesco marched impenitent and won a year in prison for his pains, I overhear a tourist family at the next table. In New Jersey cadence, the mother suggests a next day's trip to the basilica in Assisi. She sells it: "It's where St. Francis is from." Her son whines, "Who's St. Francis?" The mother pauses. The pavement birds are belled into the evening sky. "He's this really famous Franciscan monk."

*

In the basilica, the nave vaults with sky, a gloaming blue clouded with verdant green. Gold stars fan out like finches. Like gilt notes on an ethereal staff.

*

Ralph Vaughan Williams, son of a vicar, took up an old German tune "Lasst uns Erfreuen" ("Let Us Rejoice"), harmonizing his Anglican to that melody's spare Jesuit. *And how hear we every man in our own tongue, wherein we were born?*

*

It's not the repeated *alleluia*. It's not the catalogue of earthy beauty. It's not the open-throated Ptolemaic chime. What undoes me is the single minor chord.

*

Undone. Unfathered. Lazar-house. Lost. Tempest. Prison. Babel. Evening. "Sora nostra morte corporale."

*

The minor chord: unheard in the tune's Teutonic plainchants, unheard before Vaughan Williams' harmonies. It falls at the end of the penultimate line of each verse—in some versions of Draper's English text, the minored syllable is *Him*, and in some it is *Jah*; either way, God takes the fall.

Vaughan Williams' minor chord is the musical cognate of Francesco's steadfast praise in and through the death of the flesh: a gutpunch that refuses to be redeemed by the next line's joy.

Confiteor: The next line's return to D major requires a resolve that, many days, I don't have.

In the Upper Church in Assisi, the fresco cycle attributed (probably wrongly) to Giotto includes *San Francesco d'Assisi predica agli uccelli*. There are doves, of course, in the saint's congregation. There is a woodcock, I think. A robin. They will not fly until his sermon is finished. Until he follows the downpour with worms.

Nearby, another fresco shows Francis struck with stigmata; each wound an asterisk, a caveat. A flurry of wings above his head.

You lights of evening

At the altar in Assisi, my vespers are belled into the vault, where they flock and cloud.

Outside, rain. The birds tangle among the leaves, sustain their refractory antiphon. *All with one accord in one place.*

*

"perdonano per lo tue amore / infirmitate e tribulation"

*

Pardon and love, weakness and wrack. Blame and whine, and worms and no escape. *O praise Him.*

*

A creaturely hymn for us creatures: Pietro called Francesco, faux Giotto, bereft William, Ralph, the variant birds, and myself. Each of us cloven by major and minor, each our own Pentecost.

Precious Lord, Take My Hand

Precious Lord, take my hand,
lead me on, let me stand;
I am tired, I am weak, I am worn.
Through the storm, through the night,
lead me on to the light.
Take my hand, precious Lord, lead me home.

When my way grows drear,
precious Lord, linger near.
When my life is almost gone,
hear my cry, hear my call,
hold my hand, lest I fall.
Take my hand, precious Lord, lead me home.

When the darkness appears
and the night draws near,
and the day is past and gone,
at the river I stand,
guide my feet, hold my hand.
Take my hand, precious Lord, lead me home.

Thomas A. Dorsey (1899–1993)

SYDNEY LEA

SHORT TREATISE ON SLOWING DOWN

On the morning of August 20, 2016, I felt a subtle pinch in my upper torso, right side. My wife and I were at our remote cabin in Washington County, Maine, where, among other things, despite my 73 years, I'd been training for a local twelve-mile paddle race. I felt fitter than I had in recent years, when, nonetheless, and despite the fact that the contest was not divided into age classes, I'd consistently finished at or near the head of the flotilla.

The 2016 race, however, was canceled—mercifully, perhaps—for fear of lightning. I felt disappointment, but went about my business. I kept paddling hard, training a young bird dog, chopping wood, and putting things up for the winter in anticipation of our imminent departure for home. I never experienced shortness of breath, no acute pain or crushing sensation, and, but for one very brief and (then) inexplicable moment, no light-headedness. I did feel unusually tired for the ensuing day and a half, and that mosquito-like pinch in my chest persisted.

At length, given that persistence and more importantly my family history—father, grandfather, and great grandfather all dead of coronaries in their fifties—my wife and I decided I should go to the tiny clinic on the New Brunswick border. When, on looking at a blood test, the emergency room doctor informed me I was having a heart attack, I was incredulous. Those were words spoken about other people, not me.

After the three-hour ambulance ride to Bangor and some hours in which the nitroglycerine did not eliminate that little mosquito pinch, I remember being wheeled at what seemed an alarmingly fast clip to some location within the Eastern Maine Medical Center, where a stent would soon be inserted into my 100% occluded right coronary artery.

Sixteen days later, I was in cardio rehab, keeping my heart rate between 125 and 135 for forty minutes at a clip, feeling fitter than before, when I hadn't known a thing was wrong with me. Luckily, damage to the heart proved minimal, and I have felt very well ever since. No need for nitro; textbook blood pressure; in short, little to alarm me. Touch wood.

But it's that whirlwind trip to the operating room that I recall most vividly. I can't say I felt terror, because I didn't. It was something else that I can't adequately describe: I can say only that the speed of my world in its spinning unsettled me, to use an imprecise verb. I tried to study things on the corridors' ceilings—a water stain, a light fixture, a sheet rock seam, what have you—but no sooner did I fix my eye on whatever it was than it vanished.

I am one who from his middle years onward has chosen to believe in grace, by which I mean unmerited favor. That the opening of the most famous hymn composed by Thomas Dorsey, the father of gospel music, came to mind strikes me in retrospect as oddly unsurprising, though in my all-white, Vermont Congregational church this is not a hymn much heard:

> Precious Lord, take my hand,
> lead me on, let me stand,
> I am tired, I am weak, I am worn;
> through the storm, through the night,
> lead me on to the light . . .

Yet I can't logically account for why "Precious Lord" should have sung itself to me, as it were, in crisis. (If grace were logical, it wouldn't be grace.) Of course, it *is* a famous hymn, and in its rawness and directness, a perfect product of its tragic occasion. Mr. Dorsey, who beforehand was a fairly prominent purveyor of "devil's music," had confronted the death of his wife Nettie in childbirth, and, within 48 hours, the death of their baby as well. If I too felt tired, weak, and worn, as a blessed husband and father, I literally can't imagine how Georgia Tom, Dorsey's moniker in his bluesman days, must have felt in his far, far more taxing circumstance. He later spoke of how spontaneously the hymn had come to him: he simply started to sing its words.

Somehow, on hearing those very words within my soul (likely in the voice of Mahalia Jackson, who rendered them so movingly at Dr. King's funeral), I did sense that I'd somehow passed through a storm, that light shone ahead. I sensed this chiefly because that full-tilt world had abruptly *slowed down*. Indeed, things now seemed to transpire as if in cinematic slow motion.

This was not, perhaps the greatest instance of grace in my life. That surely occurred when, many years back, I found myself in abiding recovery from alcoholism. I had tried and tried to get away from alcohol and in some measure drugs and never succeeded for any length of time. Then some power greater than my puny little will mercifully intervened.

Those of us who have found sobriety by way of twelve-step programs frequently recite the so-called Serenity Prayer, attributed to Reinhold Niebuhr: *God grant me the serenity to accept the things I cannot change, courage to change the things I can, and wisdom to know the difference.* That this simple and cogent entreaty should have seamlessly introduced itself into the still, small space created by Thomas Dorsey's poignant hymn did not strike me as strange on that gurney ride.

It still doesn't. In many ways, these two prayers—one sung, the other recited—voice the same plea for comfort and resolve. To be sure, as with so many similar moments of clarity, I will forget them for stretches of the time left to me, suppressing that sense of calm and deliberation in favor of whatever idle ends I cling to even in professional retirement. But the contingency of Dorsey's hymn and Niebuhr's prayer in that hour on that day in that hospital is something that I will always own and can always refer to. I have faith that one or the other or both will be available when I most need them against the helter-skelter of so much human experience.

The same one they sold into Egypt
is the same one free them.
I say the same one they sold into Egypt
is the same one free them.
The same one they sold into Egypt
is the same one free them.
Wo-yo-yo. Wo-yo-yo.
What a ting, Selassie, what a ting.

SHARA MCCALLUM

OF PROPHECY AND DREAM

This verse is what remains in memory of a hymn I sang in childhood, at a time when I was possessed of or was possessed by a great faith. As a young girl in Kingston in the 1970s, I was raised as a member of the Twelve Tribes of Israel, the Rastafarian group to which my family belonged. While I have lived outside of this community for over thirty years and no longer practice or adhere to the belief system, lessons it imparted early on indelibly shaped me and I have carried them, as with this hymn, with me since.

The refrain—*the same one they sold into Egypt is the same one free them*—contains the whole of the story of Joseph, a tale of jealousy and its consequences, of one's ability to endure and overcome slavery and exile, of the power of prophecy and dream. Originating in the Torah, Joseph's narrative was later incorporated into and retold in The Old Testament and the Qur'an. Rastafari's 20th century adoption of this Jewish account replicates what humans have done for thousands of years—borrowed from (or often usurped) the myths of other peoples to reconstitute those as part of a new set of beliefs. With each telling of Joseph's saga, in a changed social, political, spiritual, and temporal context, Joseph has been transformed to suit the needs of the developing faith.

Who Joseph *becomes*, in the context of Twelve Tribes in the 1970s in Jamaica, is replete in the hymn's summary of his story and implicit commentary on it. Joseph was one of the youngest sons of the Jewish patriarch Jacob (who would later become *Israel*) and the most beloved of his father's children. Sibling rivalry is a leitmotif in the Torah, and Jacob's preference for Joseph. Persuaded against doing so by their youngest brother, they throw Joseph into a pit before selling him to a passing caravan of slavers. Ultimately he lands in Egypt and, through a series of further dramatic events, rises to become Vizier, second only in power to the Pharaoh himself. It is in Egypt, in exile, that Joseph goes from being the one who was betrayed to the one who saves, from slave to prophet and interpreter of dreams.

It makes perfect sense to me now, as it didn't occur when I was a child singing without the fullness of understanding, that Joseph's narrative would assume a central place in Rastafarian culture and be codified in one of our hymns. In Twelve Tribes we did not have a written text unique to our faith but developed liturgy by reading the Holy Bible and through song and prayer. Our leader Brother Gad instilled in us an understanding of scripture not only as parable, warning against human foible, but as akin to dream, containing signs for us to divine our present moment and foretell the future. Within my family, my mother read the bible aloud to me and my sisters, *a chapter a day*, explaining the stories we imbibed as allegories, written thousands and thousands of years ago to foreshadow our lives.

Joseph's story had forecasted our own experience as Jamaicans, people of largely African descent who had been sold into slavery and were now living in exile. Like Joseph, as Rastas we were charged with serving as prophets in a foreign land. And, as is often the case with prophets, we were at first neither heard nor heeded.

When Rastafari began to emerge in Jamaica in the 1930s and up until the latter part of the 20th century, Rastas were widely regarded as pariahs. They were viewed as degenerates and potentially dangerous—politically and existentially. Jamaica gained its independence from Britain in 1962, but the yoke of colonialism is not one thrown off in a singular moment or gesture. The Rastafari world view, imparted to me as a child, offered a path toward dismantling the pervading colonial world order. Not alone, but in parcel with other anti-colonialist and anti-racist movements that gathered force inside and outside of Jamaica throughout the 20th century, Rastafari as a movement helped to provide Jamaica with a different vision of ourselves as a people.

With this hymn of Joseph and others, my family and I and all our brethren and sistren in Twelve Tribes were prophesying this vision. In word and deed, we opposed the culture's worship of a system of economics that lacks moral compass, evidenced in the grotesquery of slavery. Staunchly anti-capitalist, we advocated for wealth redistribution as a way to work toward achieving social justice. Confronted by colonialism and racism, we rejected the premise of social hierarchy on which those systems are predicated and preached equality across class and racial lines (gender, I'm afraid, was somewhat of an oversight). Twelve Tribes included many mixed-race families like my own, but we recognized that it was the African in us that had been systematically denigrated and we looked toward the continent for self-worth, self-definition, and safe haven, the goal of repatriation being strong in Twelve Tribes when I was a child. Tuning our ear to the prophetic and messianic strains of Judaism and Christianity, we carried those into our present—identifying a contemporary African leader as the incarnation of God.

For Rastas in Twelve Tribes, Haile Selassie I, Regent of Ethiopia from 1916-1930 and Emperor from 1930-1974, was seen as an avatar of the divine—in the same way Jesus was and is believed by his followers to be the embodiment of God. In our greetings we affirmed this deeply held conviction: *I greet you in the name of His Imperial Majesty, H.I.M., who has been made known to us in the flesh in the form of Haile Selassie I, King of Kings, Lord of Lords, Conquering Lion of the Tribe of Judah.* I was three years old in 1975, the year Selassie died, yet throughout my childhood in Jamaica I called out to, praised, and celebrated HIM—*Jah, Rastafari, Selassie I*—as did all the members of my community

Prophecy and prophesying were pivotal to the fabric of the world I understood as a child, woven into such daily acts as this greeting and manifest in larger ways. In my memory, my family and community lived with a sense of impending Armageddon, which would be brought on by man's continued inhumanity to man and was especially present in the threat of nuclear war and devastation we feared would soon befall civilization. All this was foretold by the stories of the Jewish and Christian bibles, written down more than two-thousand years ago. Faced with these signs, like Joseph and other prophets of the biblical texts, we were to use words and reason to warn of the downfalls of the past and present and to *chant down Babylon.*

Though as a child I could not comprehend the fullness of the hymn's meaning, I think now it helped inculcate in me the belief that knowledge of suffering should lead us to something greater: to become like Joseph and to prophesy in another sense of that word. To speak of what we see, not only for our own benefit but also for the sake of others. It is a complex speech act we are asked to perform when we prophesy: one that registers our own pain—*wo-yo-yo, wo-yo-yo*, the lament in the hymn's response to the call of the refrain sounds this, the grief of exile and of being betrayed. But prophesying is also an act of speaking that conveys gratitude and wonderment—*what a ting*—at the gifts adversity and struggle can paradoxically instill in us: generosity, compassion, and a sense of our own power in the face of apparent powerlessness.

At the end of the story, when famine is upon the land, Joseph's brothers are forced to travel to Egypt seeking food. Standing before their brother, they do not recognize him and Joseph initially cannot bring himself to disclose his true identity, so ravaged is he twenty years later by grief. What a painful irony that the one who was forsaken by his brothers is the same one who would become their salvation. But what a marvel it is as well that the role Joseph is cast into is one he readily accepts and through which he understands and gleans a sense of greater purpose. *What a ting* that prophecy and dream have the power not only to deliver Joseph from enslavement and exile but to deliver his brothers who had betrayed him, to deliver the Egyptians who had enslaved him—all of them. *What a ting* indeed.

A Mighty Fortress Is Our God

A mighty fortress is our God,
a bulwark never failing;
our helper he amid the flood
of mortal ills prevailing.
For still our ancient foe
doth seek to work us woe;
his craft and power are great,
and armed with cruel hate,
on earth is not his equal.

Did we in our own strength confide,
our striving would be losing,
were not the right man on our side,
the man of God's own choosing.
Dost ask who that may be?
Christ Jesus, it is he,
Lord Sabaoth, his name,
from age to age the same,
and he must win the battle.

And though this world, with devils filled,
should threaten to undo us,
we will not fear, for God hath willed
his truth to triumph through us.
The Prince of Darkness grim,
we tremble not for him;
his rage we can endure,
for lo, his doom is sure;
one little word shall fell him.

That word above all earthly powers,
no thanks to them, abideth;
the Spirit and the gifts are ours,
thru him who with us sideth.
Let goods and kindred go,
this mortal life also;
the body they may kill;
God's truth abideth still;
his kingdom is forever.

Martin Luther (1483–1546)
Translated by Frederick Hedge (1805–1890)

MAURICE MANNING

A CATHOLIC LOVE FOR A PROTESTANT HYMN

My experience of organized religion and an active spiritual life has often asked me to accept ambiguity. I have never doubted the presence and the work of the Creator. Instead, I have doubted my own ability to understand that presence and to live with it, especially if the full meaning of that presence remains evasive. Yet this inherent discord, which seems natural and necessary, is, in my view, a pretty good claim for faith.

And faith, regardless of one's religion or denomination, is where most of us find ourselves. Faith is the realm that asks us to think, to work, to be active, to be patient, and to accept our entry into the unknown. We blindly agree something will come of it, even if what comes is wholly inscrutable. What a strange task to grab hold of! And yet, if I look around where I live and reflect on my upbringing, there seems no greater task. We should, after all, be seeking some fulfillment of being alive, to understand the purpose of life, and to make something useful of our lives. And then I ask, how many people in our troubled world really enjoy the privilege of entertaining such thoughts? That cuts me down a notch or two. So it is. I could ponder all of this till the cows come home. At some point, though, you have to get going and see what happens, a predicament not unlike that faced by a poet staring at an empty page.

I was raised in a Disciples of Christ church, a denomination that split from the Presbyterians in the early 1800s during the Second Great Awakening movement. I like to think the Disciples of Christ is a frontier denomination, parallel in many ways to the founding and design of our country—independent and separate. The Disciples of Christ was also founded in Kentucky, our nation's first frontier state, and a state my ancestors settled, so my affiliation with this denomination is natural and inherited from many generations.

When I was growing up, going to church was simply part of life. I took it seriously and I valued it. As an adult, however, I have felt maintaining an active faith, rather than a specific affiliation, is more my practice, and that has meant always a search. I have attended churches of many stripes: various evangelical churches (including Holiness churches), Southern Baptist, Episcopal, Methodist, and Catholic. In my early 20s I was a graduate student and lived in a one-room schoolhouse that had been converted to a humble residence. Living there I attended what I like to call a country Catholic church, a church in rural Kentucky absent of all formality, that included congregants who were local farmers and Hispanic immigrants. I truly felt at home at that church. No fanfare, no adornment to be seen.

I've since preferred a plain approach in any church I've attended. We presently attend a small Catholic church that was originally founded as an African-American parish. Although my wife and I have not officially converted to Catholicism, our somewhat renegade priest happily baptized our young daughter. It's all a rough fit, I'm afraid, and some of that probably has to do with my temperament; some of it is also connected to my inclinations as a poet.

It is therefore not surprising to me that one of my favorite hymns was composed by the great Protestant, Martin Luther. "A Mighty Fortress Is Our God" is a hymn that drew me into it when I was a child. I liked the words, translated into a version of English that was more or less Victorian, and must have seemed elevated to my young ears. But I liked much more the strange rhythm of the hymn. There is such a brief pause between the phrases they nearly fall on top of each other. While the melody moves forward it also jumps or bumps—it isn't a sweet or smooth movement. I can think this way as an adult; as a youngster I expect I just noted there was something strange in the music of this hymn and I liked it for that. And "A Mighty Fortress Is Our God" is a melody I've hummed to myself often through the years. I've found that in doing a chore—working in the garden, for instance, or walking in the woods—my body falls into a rhythm, and that puts my thoughts in rhythm, and pretty soon I'm humming a tune in my mind. Often—inexplicably to me other than the possibility of the strange rhythm—the tune I hum is Luther's old Reformation hit.

Yet, my experience with this hymn has a more haunting connection. In the early summer of 2011 my wife and I were bicycling on the country roads around us. A couple of weeks before we'd had a miscarriage. It was just one of those things. We were newly married, but we were in our 40s and we'd agreed that having children was an unlikely prospect. Then to our great surprise we learned Amanda was pregnant, and far enough along that we could hear a heartbeat on a visit to the doctor. A couple of weeks later we went back for another visit and an ultrasound. The technician ran the wand over Amanda's belly a few times and quietly looked up at us and said, "I'm sorry, but there isn't a heartbeat." We were stunned, and walked out into the bright day, not sure what to say or how to feel.

I have spent much of my adult life believing I am not worthy of Grace, yet time and time again it has managed to find me despite my perverse doubt. And so, a couple of weeks after the miscarriage we took a morning bicycle ride in the countryside around us. We were climbing a steep hill, about to enter the small village of Mackville. As I was pumping my way up the hill I began humming "A Mighty Fortress Is Our God," I expect simply so the rhythm of the song would drive me on. As we entered Mackville a church bell began ringing, signaling that it was noon. I looked over in a field and saw a black horse making his way to a spring for a drink. Just as the horse reached the spring, the church bell stopped. The timing of the two events struck me, and I felt a grief pass out of my being, and knew the grief was over our miscarriage. While the grief was not at that moment wholly removed, I realized I would at least come to understand it in time, or I would learn how to live with it. There was a comfort in that moment—a mysterious, foggy sense of comfort and transformation, which is often the character of my spiritual encounters.

Later that evening, I found myself drafting a poem to reflect on the events of the day. Once I got to a resting place for the poem I wondered what sort of title suited it and consulted an old hymnal to revisit the English translation of Martin Luther's words. "Amid the flood of mortal ills prevailing" immediately stood out, and that is the title of the poem in its final version. The poem appears in my most recent book, *One Man's Dark*.

Grace found us again, however, in 2015 when our daughter Lillian was born—certainly a miracle. By this time we were even older, yet had the wisdom of loss behind us, though even as I write the word, wisdom doesn't seem quite right. We are simply still learning, both from grief and joy. I am prepared to believe we are called to such a task, and certainly believe music helps to get us there.

AMID THE FLOOD OF MORTAL ILLS PREVAILING

The church bell tells the noon
and heat waves down the ridge
and one leaf, like an old man
caught in a fit, slaps itself
in the shade, and soon the black horse
slick and shiny raises his head
and wades into the tall grass
like a shadow entering a dream.
There is little motion now except
the horse and the splash of butterflies
thrown up behind it like yellow froth
wrung from the winding course of green.
And where is the black horse bound?
For the smudge of mud and water below
the willow tree where the rock mouth
hangs open underneath the hill
and the old insistent spring comes out.
Some people would say this is a dream,
and everything I've summoned here
is a symbol. But some would say it's real.
I say it's real—the sleepy heat,
the thirst, the song of country bells,
and how the horse reaches the spring
when the last bell's note is ended,
and a late sorrow goes out of me.

Three times line up, you see?
But the going out is how I know
I didn't do the summoning.

I Love to Tell the Story

I love to tell the story
of unseen things above,
of Jesus and his glory,
of Jesus and his love.
I love to tell the story,
because I know 'tis true;
it satisfies my longing
as nothing else can do.

Refrain:
I love to tell the story,
'twill be my theme in glory,
to tell the old, old story
of Jesus and his love.

I love to tell the story;
'tis pleasant to repeat
what seems, each time I tell it,
more wonderfully sweet.
I love to tell the story,
for some have never heard
the message of salvation
from God's own Holy Word.

I love to tell the story,
for those who know it best
seem hungering and thirsting
to hear it, like the rest.
And when in scenes of glory
I sing the new, new song,

'twill be the old, old story,
that I have loved so long.

Katherine Hankey (1834–1911)

KATHLEEN NORRIS

"I LOVE TO TELL THE STORY"

When I was a child I thought my family went to church in order to sing, an easy assumption, as my father was a choir director and I made my debut in a "cherub choir" at the age of four. Later, as I prepared for confirmation, I discovered that the catechism made less sense to me than the hymns I sang on Sunday morning. That's where the poetry was, and theology in a form I could understand, that enticed me on an emotional level.

The hymns I cherish most are those that combine good theology with graceful verse. "Come Down, O Love Divine," for example, with its submission to the workings of the spirit: "O let it freely burn, / till earthly passions turn / to dust and ashes in its heat consuming." I feel a pang in admitting that "the yearning strong, / for which the soul will long, / shall far outpace the power of human telling." As "human telling" is what I do, those words can be painful, but they also heal, tempering my pride.

I once used a hymn to help heal my husband. Raised a Catholic before Vatican II, he had a strained relationship with the Christian faith. He knew Reform theology—he'd read more Calvin than I had—but wasn't familiar with Protestant hymns. When I was preparing a worship service for a Presbyterian church in western South Dakota, where I would be preaching, I chose a hymn, "Immortal, Invisible, God Only Wise," with him in mind. I'm not sure my poet husband heard a word of my sermon, but after church he raved about that hymn. He recognized it as a perfect poem, by Coleridge's definition, "the best words in the best order," with its evocation of God as "unresting, unhasting, and silent as light."

As a Benedictine oblate called to daily remind myself that I am going to die, I treasure this hymn's realism: "We blossom and flourish like leaves on the tree, / then wither and perish, but naught changeth Thee." This verse holds more meaning for me as I've grown older and so many of my loved ones, including my husband, have died. The hymn ends on a mystical note about our limitations in comprehending the divine: "All laud we would render, O help us to see, / 'tis only the splendor of light hideth Thee."

I find that the best hymns are like scripture in that their words strike my heart when I most need them. If I'm experiencing spiritual dryness, the honesty of "Come Thou Fount of Every Blessing" is a balm. "Prone to wander, Lord, I feel it; / prone to leave the Lord I love." Oh, yes: preach it, brother. And when I was preparing a funeral service for my sister Rebecca, Isaac Watts' magnificent version of Psalm 23, "My Shepherd Will Supply My Need," came to mind. Brain-damaged at birth, my sister had an exceptionally difficult life, and the closing verse, with its promise of being "no more a stranger, nor a guest, / but like a child at home," seemed right.

I'd call "I Love to Tell the Story" my favorite hymn for two reasons: its simplicity, and the fact that "I love to tell the story" could be any writer's mantra. The hymn is apparently too simple for the Episcopal hymnal, which is ironic, as its author, Katherine Hankey, was a member of the "Clapham sect," a 19th-century group of evangelical Anglicans devoted to ending slavery. My copy comes from a Presbyterian hymnal.

I appreciate the line "those who know it best / seem hungering and thirsting / to hear it, like the rest" as a challenge. Any writer knows the value of repetition, but here it is deemed essential to a faith that can never be fully grasped or mastered. All we can do is listen to the story once again, and allow it to become fresh and new.

Even as a child I was attracted to this hymn's insistence on the vast import of story: the idea that hearing and telling Bible stories involved me in something much larger than I could comprehend, that transcended time itself. And this makes the hymn's last verse difficult for me to sing without weeping: "And when in scenes of glory / I sing the new, new song, / 'twill be the old, old story, / that I have loved so long."

One of the miracles of people singing hymns together is that they can transform even a drab hotel conference room into a bit of heaven. This hymn asserts that heaven is indeed full of singing and encourages me to envision all the people I have loved being with me there and joining in. And we'll discover that the new song we're singing is the gospel in a nutshell, that "old, old story, of Jesus and his love."

Biographical note:

I was raised in Methodist and UCC churches, and, even though I'm not sure this is allowed, I am currently a member of a Presbyterian church in my mother's home town in South Dakota, and in an Episcopal church in Honolulu. In 1987 I became an oblate of a Benedictine monastery, Assumption Abbey, in western North Dakota.

Come, My Beloved, to Greet the Bride; Let Us Welcome the Shabbat

Come, my Beloved, to meet the Bride; let us welcome the Shabbat.

"Observe" and "Remember," the one and only G-d caused us to hear in a single utterance; the L-rd is One and His Name is One, for renown, for glory and for praise.

Come, my Beloved . . .

Come, let us go to welcome the Shabbat, for it is the source of blessing; from the beginning, from aforetime, it was chosen; last in creation, first in [G-d's] thought.

Come, my Beloved . . .

Sanctuary of the King, royal city, arise, go forth from the ruins; too long have you dwelt in the vale of tears; He will show you abounding mercy.

Come, my Beloved . . .

Shake the dust off yourself, arise, don your glorious garments, my people. Through the son of Yishai of Bet Lechem, draw near to my soul and redeem it.

Come, my Beloved . . .

Arouse yourself, arouse yourself, for your light has come; arise, shine. Awake, awake, utter a song; the glory of the L-rd is revealed upon you.

Come, my Beloved . . .

Do not be ashamed nor confounded; why are you downcast and why are you agitated? The afflicted of my people will find refuge in you; the city will be rebuilt on its former site.

Come, my Beloved . . .

Those who despoil you will be despoiled, and all who would destroy you will be far away. Your G-d will rejoice over you as a bridegroom rejoices over his bride.

Come, my Beloved . . .

To the right and to the left you shall spread out, and the L-rd you shall extol. And we shall rejoice and exult, through the man who is a descendant of Peretz.

Come, my Beloved . . .

Come in peace, O crown of her Husband, both with songs and gladness; among the faithful, the beloved people, come, O Bride, come, O Bride.

Come, my Beloved . . .

Rabbi Shlomo HaLevi Alkabetz (c. 1500–1576)

YEHOSHUA NOVEMBER

"COME, MY BELOVED, TO GREET THE BRIDE; LET US WELCOME THE SHABBAT"

Narrow arches and walkways opening to private gardens, white linens on rooftop clothes lines, ancient stone synagogues, the holy Wailing Wall itself. When I was eighteen, I spent a year in the Old City of Jerusalem. I had just broken up with a girlfriend and graduated from a public school in Pittsburgh, the former steel-mill city whose working-class population idolizes the Steelers and Penguins. Now, I found myself in an all-male yeshiva, my dorm room only several hundred yards from Judaism's most sacred site. Though situated at the heart of my people's history, I felt far away, geographically and spiritually.

To be sure, I had grown up in a traditional Jewish home. We observed the Sabbath and followed Jewish dietary laws. But it was a home that placed equal—if not more—emphasis on the arts and secular culture. As I write in one of my poems, the Marx Brothers' movies served as background to family dinners, and Sam Cooke's sensual voice would float up from my father's Danish speakers when he returned home after a long day of seeing patients. My mother was a student of art history. Biographies of artists lined our shelves, and Impressionist prints hung on the walls. On road trips, my father played Bob Dylan, Leonard Cohen, The Drifters, Roy Orbison, and Marty Robbins (my first exposure to poetry). Indeed, I had spent most of my life in Jewish day schools. I had even completed close to a year of studies in a yeshiva in Rochester—a far more zealous institution than the school in Jerusalem, where students didn't dress solely in black and white and were encouraged to attend secular universities. Still, on the cusp of adulthood, in a distant environment devoted exclusively to Judaic studies, I felt more keenly a tension I had always felt: the pull between the here and now and the spiritual afterlife, which, as the rabbis of my youth had so often underscored, awaits those strong enough to jettison their worldly concerns and devote themselves to Torah study. That year, I learned a few pages of a Talmudic tractate on marriage but also found a small used book store in the Jewish Quarter where I purchased *The Brothers Karamazov*, *Jude the Obscure*, and Malamud's *The Fixer*. I also wrote the sort of bad poetry only a perplexed 18-year-old can write, and did not fail to notice the young women from London attending a seminary around the corner from our yeshiva.

Every Friday night, as the sun set over Jerusalem, arms over each other's shoulders, the students at the yeshiva danced down the long set of stone steps that led to the Western Wall, where we would pray the service that welcomes in the Sabbath. Our enigmatic head rabbi—a stocky man with a high-pitched voice—criticized this ritual as too demonstrative, an attempt to get ourselves photographed by the many tourists who'd come to visit the holy site. Perhaps he was right, but I remember these moments as a point of light and clarity in a confusing time. And as I danced with my classmates—many of whom I secretly resented for their profuse praises of the yeshiva staff and their readiness to dive into the Torah's waters—I sensed a kind of peace wash over me.

At the bottom of the steps we formed a circle and danced in front of the ancient Wall whose cracks were crammed with desperate notes—scribbled prayers for healing, for an escape from poverty, for children, for finally finding the fated marriage partner. A classmate with a sweet voice would take his spot in the front of our group and begin to lead the Sabbath evening prayers. Soon, the sky overhead turned deep blue, and we sang the hymn that ushers in the Sabbath, "Come, My Beloved, to Greet the Bride. Let Us Welcome the Shabbat." I didn't know it at the time, but this mystical poem—especially when read according to Hasidic thought—complicates the theology that sees this physical life solely as a means to a later spiritual reward. As I hope to explain, the poem turns upside down a worldview that prizes the Heavens over the Divine possibilities of the everyday. And, for me at least, this reversal seems to run parallel to the tendency of many contemporary poets to locate transcendence and light not in the sublime moment but in the mundane.

Over the years, I've heard "Come, My Beloved, to Greet the Bride," which likens the Sabbath to both a bride and a queen, put to many different tunes. (I even know of a rendition that uses Simon and Garfunkel's "Scarborough Fair" as melody). The lyrics, however, were composed by a 16th-century Kabbalist, Rabbi Shlomo HaLevi Alkabetz, who lived in Safed, a city in Northern Israel where the great Kabbalists of that time converged. In acrostic fashion, the poet's name, Shlomo HaLevi, Solomon the Levite, is woven into the first letters of the poem's first eight stanzas. It's said that many mystics in Safed composed Sabbath poems during this period, but only "Come, My Beloved" won the deep admiration of Rabbi Isaac Luria, the father of Lurianic Kabbalah and the leading Jewish mystic of Alkabetz's era.

Each Friday evening, as the sun set, Luria and his students would go out to the Galilean Hills to read from the Psalms and welcome in the Sabbath. Tradition has it that these excursions inspired Alkabetz to compose "Come, My Beloved." The poem became the seventh hymn the mystics recited during their services under the open sky, corresponding to the seventh day of the Jewish week, the Sabbath. (Luria and his colleagues preceded "Come, My Beloved" with the recitation of six chapters from the Psalms, each one corresponding to one of the six days of creation). On Friday nights, many Jewish communities across the world continue to recite this seven-hymn formula initiated in 16th-century Safed. And Alkebetz's poem remains one of the few prayers composed as late as it was in Jewish history to be included in Jewish prayer books across all denominations.

Our yeshiva's effort to usher in the Sabbath with a heightened sense of ceremony clearly dates back to Alkabetz's time. But key phrases in Alkabetz's poem—as well as the mystics' practice of going out to the hills to pray—owe something to the Talmudic sages who lived more than a thousand years prior to the Jewish mystics of the 1500s. The Talmud notes that each Friday evening, two rabbis, Rebbi Hanina and Rebbi Yanai, would don elegant robes as the sun set. Rebbi Hanina would say, "Come let us go and greet the Sabbath Queen." Rebbi Yanai would proclaim, "Enter, O bride! Enter, O bride!" (Tractate Sabbath 119:A). Alkabetz borrows from Rebbi Hanina's pronouncement in the poem's refrain, which also serves as the poem's first line, and Rebbi Yanai's words appear in the final stanza. Interestingly, as they recite this final verse, contemporary worshippers turn to the back of the synagogue, to the doorway, a gesture that signifies welcoming in the Sabbath presence and recalls the practice of exiting the synagogue to pray under the sky.

In a basic reading of the poem, the first two stanzas and the final one praise the Sabbath and call upon the reader and/or G-d to welcome the day with joy and eagerness. The middle stanzas articulate a longing for the end of the long Jewish exile (which began in 70 CE, with the destruction of the Second Temple). In stanza three, Alkabetz addresses this theme directly: "Sanctuary of the King, royal city . . . / too long have you dwelt in the vale of tears."

When I completed my studies in Jerusalem, I returned to the States to concentrate on poetry. Of all times and places, it was as an MFA student, married and back in Pittsburgh, that I first encountered the Hasidic mystical teachings, including those that focus on Alkabetz's poem. In particular, I found myself drawn to the Hasidic claim—based in Midrash—that all of creation, including the loftiest Heavens, was constructed because G-d desires a home in this lowest realm, in our mundane world. The Jewish mystics explain that the fulfillment of each Divine command, or mitzvah, draws an infinite Divine light down to this physical reality, refining and uplifting the material world. According to Hasidic thought, this process will culminate in the Messianic Era, when all physical reality has been refined and can serve as a vessel to reveal the Divine unity underlying creation—a home for G-d in the lower realm. The Sabbath, when the Divinity behind the world's curtain is less concealed, is said to be a foretaste of that era.

If in Jerusalem my pendulum swung toward poetry and the secular, in graduate school for poetry, it swung toward Hasidic philosophy. I became so enchanted by this mystical tradition that I enrolled in a Hasidic yeshiva as soon as I finished my MFA. I thought I was turning my back on poetry and academia (which appeared to leave little room for Hasidic life), that I would become a rabbi and perhaps give up on poetry entirely. Ultimately, it was the Hasidic texts themselves, along with the advice of a good mentor, that helped me see things in less dichotomous terms—that helped me realize I could attempt to live as a Hasid and, at the same time, as a poet and writing professor in university.

Similarly, seen through a mystical lens—especially that of Hasidic mysticism—Alkebetz's poem appears to offer a theology that contrasts with the bifurcated notion of Judaism I had encountered—and felt alienated from—in my youth. It offers a world-embracing version of Jewish life and the universe, going as far as to take a mystical form of love making (which, according to Hasidic thought, serves as the source of physical intimacy between husband and wife) as its central allusion. The poem celebrates the Sabbath as a sort of restful glorification of the Divine energy responsible for finitude and physicality and suggests that this energy has something to offer the Divine spheres associated with G-d's infinity and transcendence (spheres synonymous with the afterlife I had been told to strive for as an endgame). In the poem's refrain, Alkabetz enjoins the "Beloved" to engage with the "Bride." The mystics note that the term "Beloved" derives from Song of Songs, where it connotes G-d's masculine or infinite attributes. G-d as He transcends the world. In contrast, "Bride" refers to the Shechina, or G-d's feminine posture, that energy invested in and responsible for perpetuation of the finite and the physical.

In a Hasidic discourse on Alkabetz's poem, likely delivered shortly before the beginning of the 19th century, Rabbi Schneur Zalman of Liadi, the Alter Rebbe, explains that on the Sabbath G-d's transcendent, masculine energy, the Beloved, lowers itself to lift up the feminine finite energy, the Bride, which is invested in creation throughout the week. Alkabetz alludes to this process in the first part of the poem's refrain: "Come, My Beloved to greet the Bride." The Beloved then draws the Bride—along with all of creation—back to its source in the upper spiritual worlds, representing a kind of Sabbath or respite. (The Hebrew word for Sabbath actually derives from the Hebrew term for return—in this case the Shechina returns to the upper worlds, to Its source). The "Beloved" then spiritually inseminates the "Bride" with a new Divine light. As a literal translation of the refrain continues, "The faces of the Sabbath let us welcome." The Hebrew word for faces—Pnai—is rooted in the word Panimiyus, which means internal or within. Here, then, Alkabetz alludes to the mystical Bride's absorption of the mystical Beloved's spiritual "seed," or Divine light, a kind of internal Sabbath, a restoration of energies that ultimately leads to the "birth" of another week.

However, as noted, in Hasidic thought, the physical world—associated with Shechina—is the stage on which creation's ultimate purpose plays out. The higher worlds serve as a sort of spiritual bridge down to physical reality. As such, according to the Alter Rebbe, Alkebetz's phrasing implies that the transcendent, masculine light—Beloved—also experiences a kind of Sabbath, a return to, and infusion from, its source, but only once it has infused the Shechina with new life. Hence the plural wording, "The *faces* of the Sabbath let *Us* welcome." On the Sabbath, the masculine, infinite energy (along with, and for the sake of, the Bride) enjoys its re-vivification. It too is lifted back to a higher place in the Heavens and receives and internalizes a new Divine flow of energy. The Alter Rebbe adds that, according to Alkabetz, it appears G-d's infinite, masculine energy and G-d's feminine, finite mode enjoy equal footing on the Sabbath, both greeting "the faces of Sabbath"—a return to a higher spiritual realm—together. Elsewhere, the Alter Rebbe explains that, in the Messianic Era, when physicality has been fully refined and spiritualized, the two energies will share equal standing throughout the week, and in the end, G-d's feminine attribute—which plays a more central role in making the physical world a home for G-d—will prove superior.

As a poet and a student of Hasidic thought, it has been illuminating to take note of the overlap between contemporary poetry and the Hasidic endeavor to sanctity the quotidian. Though contemporary poetry is generally seen as a secular enterprise, the impulse to elevate the mundane, to shine light on the ordinary, also appears to drive many contemporary poets. For some, it is poetry's central ambition (just look at the lines of praise on the jacket of most volumes of contemporary poetry). Alkabetz's poem celebrates the Sabbath, a day when the ordinary, the finite, is not overlooked or degraded, but lifted up and infused with transcendent light. It would seem that—albeit in a secular sense—many contemporary poets observe a kind of Sabbath, shining luminous light on our finite lives, directing our gaze not up toward the Heavens but down toward the sacred possibilities of our earthly existence.

Psalm 115:17–18

The dead don't praise God and the ones who go down to silence.
But we'll bless God from now on forever. Hallelujah.

translation by Jacqueline Osherow

The dead praise not the LORD, neither any that go down into silence.
But we will bless the LORD from this time forth and for evermore. Praise the
Lord.

King James Version

Psalm 118:5

From a narrow place I called to God; He answered me from the wideness of
God.

translation by Jacqueline Osherow

I called upon the Lord in distress: the Lord answered me, and set me in a large
place.

King James Version

Psalm 118:24

This is the day the Lord has made; we shall rejoice and be happy in it.

translation by Jacqueline Osherow

This is the day which the Lord hath made; we will rejoice and be glad in it.

King James Version

JACQUELINE OSHEROW

THREE VERSES FROM HALLEL

"From the narrow place, I called out to God; He answered me from the wideness of God." I offer this somewhat homely, literal translation of Psalm 118, verse 5, because it seems to me—in its beautiful Hebrew, if not this clunky English version—to encapsulate what poetry is (or, at least, what it can be) more succinctly, powerfully, and incontrovertibly than any other line of poetry I know. The verse acknowledges the impossibility of its project while nonetheless embarking on it; the words insist on their ability to get from the particular—one's own hopelessly narrow human place—out into vastness. Isn't this always, to some degree, poetry's project? Doesn't the poet always, in one way or another, cry out from his or her narrow place, hoping for some broader, wider resonance, for the most ample imaginable response?

The King James is not inaccurate in rendering the verse: "I called upon the Lord in distress: the Lord answered me, and set me in a large place." Like so many Hebrew words, meitzar (distress, narrowness, narrow place, strait) goes in a number of different but related directions. In modern Hebrew, the word, in its verb form, means "to regret." It's also related to the name for Egypt—mitzrayim—which can be understood to mean something like "double narrowness" or "double trouble." That the King James, at least this time, renders anani as "He answered me" is a great thing. In all too many instances in the book of Psalms—even in verse 21 of this same Psalm—the King James inexplicably translates the word "He heard me," making God passive instead of active and removing what may well be my favorite feature of the psalms: God's active collaboration in them. In Hebrew, the Psalms give the impression—at least to me—of managing, by calling upon God so insistently and exquisitely from however narrow a starting point, to invoke God, in all His ampleness, into existence. Their "call" finally elicits God's response until He seems to participate in their own making.

Did I recognize any of this when I finally began to realize—probably as an adolescent—that I actually understood a number of these verses of psalms I had been singing on every major holiday (and new moon, when it happened to fall on a Saturday) in synagogue for so many years? I doubt it. I'm not sure I even knew the words came from the Psalms. Nor am I sure how it is that I understood them. By listening to announcements in Hebrew at summer camp? From Hebrew school, where, from the age of nine, we were given simplified Biblical texts to read in Hebrew, each chapter with its own enormous glossary? All I know is how thrilling it was suddenly to recognize that I could derive literal meaning from "min hameitzar karati ya; anani ba merchav ya" ("From the narrow place . . . "), and I promptly fell in love with it. It is—like so many lines of Psalms—beautifully direct and fairly simple in Hebrew. But I doubt that I understood its implications. Still, every time I read it, it gave me the most wonderful sense of possibility. And I quickly came to see that any line I sang from Hallel would reward me enormously, if only I paid attention. Ordinarily this would be a big if, given my still unchecked tendency to blab shamelessly in the back row during services. But I make an exception for Hallel.

Hallel, meaning praise—the short service added to the morning prayers on holidays and new moons—contains Psalms 113 through 118 and has always been my favorite service, even before I understood it. I loved its sounds and the many lovely melodies used to sing them. But little did I know how revelatory it was and would continue to be. Even after understanding the Hebrew words was second nature to me, a verse could always astonish me.

Perhaps the most memorable occasion was on Shavuot, 1991. I was enormously sad, having just learned from a dear friend about his sister's death—a week after she'd given birth to her first child—from an undetected congenital heart defect. When, during Hallel, I sang out, "This is the day which the Lord has made; we will be rejoice and be glad in it" (Psalm 118:24 KJV), the familiar line seemed to explode. There was, after all, a new baby, who deserved someone's joy, despite the terrible loss associated with his birth. And this demand that one live well, indeed joyfully, with what one could not change, struck me as something to cling to in those tragic circumstances. Since then, I've clung to it many times. It still seems like a most difficult imperative, this requirement to rejoice in days so profoundly imperfect, and so very much not of our own making. But it also strikes me as one we would all do well to fulfill.

And Hallel does seem to insist that its own enterprise, praising God, is among the most straightforward and dependable ways to fulfill it. Indeed, in Hallel, praising God is likened to life itself, even eternal life: "The dead praise not the LORD, neither any that go down into silence. / But we will bless the LORD from this time forth and for evermore. Praise the Lord (Hallelujah)" (Psalm 115:17–18 KJV). Again, we have a tight collaboration: God keeps us alive so we can keep His praises alive and in so doing tap into God's own eternity. This praise of God that can bring us from mortality to eternity is a sort of temporal analogue to the calling out to God that brings us from narrowness to amplitude. Here we not only insist and affirm God into existence, but ourselves "from this time forth and for evermore." An exultant "Hallelujah" seals the deal. This word itself—literally a plural imperative to praise God—is the human route from limitation to boundlessness. And from the tragedy that is so often a result of that human limitation to rejoicing. For me—even now—it's the most magical exemplar of that breathtaking concept: holy language, which, along with all the exquisite intimations that holy language can introduce but never quite contain, is surely what made me long, from my earliest days, to try my hand at writing poems.

Amazing Grace

Amazing grace, how sweet the sound
that saved a wretch like me!
I once was lost, but now am found,
was blind, but now I see.

'Twas grace that taught my heart to fear,
and grace that fear relieved;
how precious did that grace appear
the hour I first believed.

Through many trials, toils, and snares
we have already come.
'Twas grace that brought us safe thus far,
and grace will lead us home.

When we've been there ten thousand years,
bright shining as the sun,
we've no less days to sing God's praise
than when we first begun.

John Newton (1725–1807)

ALICIA OSTRIKER

"AMAZING GRACE": SINGER AND SONG

"There is another world, but it is within this one."
–Paul Eluard

I like to sing. Singing, like poetry, enables us to enter experiences other than our own. I sing lively Elizabethan songs by Thomas Campion, melancholy ones by John Dowland, gems from Shakespeare's plays, "Greensleeves," and the medieval "Cherry Tree Carol" in which a pregnant Mary confronts an angry Joseph, and an unborn Jesus solves the conflict. I sing popular songs from the '30s, learned from my parents. Does anybody remember "A Bicycle Built for Two?" Then there are show tunes, folk songs, protest songs, spirituals, blues. I liked to belt out "Can't Help Lovin' That Man of Mine" when I was six or seven and had no idea what it was all about. When my dad came home after union meetings, we used to sing "Oh you can't scare me, I'm stickin' to the Union," banging our fists on the table. In chorus in high school we sang Fauré's "Requiem" and I thought it was the most beautiful thing I ever heard. In chorus in college we sang Beethoven's Ninth, and I could climb up to high C with the rest of the sopranos and sail along there as long as Beethoven and Schiller needed me to.

Once I could sing along with the Queen of the Night in "Die Zauberflote." Those were the days. Now I am a moderately passable alto in my local amateur chorus. I'll sing in the shower, doing dishes, hiking, biking. I sang in my head when I was in labor. I'll sing in my head when I'm sleepless. The text might be Yeats' "The Song of Wandering Aengus," brimful of longing. It might be cool Bob Dylan, slick Joni Mitchell, or magical Leonard Cohen.

The dimension of spirituality in poetry and song has always drawn me into it. Why is that? My lefty Jewish family raised me to be an atheist; my spiritual training consisted of being told that religion was the opiate of the masses; never have I literally experienced anything that might be called "belief" or "faith" in a personal God. The violent and punitive God worshipped in Judeo–Christian traditions is a figure I have wrestled with in book after book. And yet the idea of a world of the spirit existing within, or beneath, the material world, the world of our bodies, seems real to me. Not above us, dispensing rewards and punishments. Nothing to do with dogma.

The one hymn in my repertoire is "Amazing Grace." Part of what's lovely to me about "Amazing Grace" is the melody, those smooth waves rising and resolving. Partly it is the sweetness of an achieved serenity, in which a "lost" and "blind" past has been absorbed, into a present that ripples with goodness and peacefulness.

As a pinch of salt accentuates a dish's sweetness, or a dash of black makes a gallon of white paint more vividly white, the song makes me appreciate being found as a child in a game of lost-and-found might appreciate it, or as a child who has accidentally strayed might be extra grateful when family shows up and dinner is waiting. Although the song does not explicitly say so, to be lost to oneself, and there are so many ways for that to happen, and then to have found oneself, is to be at ease in body and mind. Blindness, though—or so it seems to me—is something one wills. A hardness, an armoring of the self, a deliberate not-knowing, not-feeling. A refusal to recognize reality. We all suffer some blindness, and we know we do, and can't help it.

Grace does the helping, the achieving, the accomplishing. Amazing grace, with its lovely assonance, surrounds us with safety and enlightens our minds. We need do nothing, it just happens—happens miraculously. Grace touches the heart and teaches it to fear—fear what? Punishment, eternal punishment? Or staying lost forever, without a family? Or being mired in self-hatred? Yet almost the instant this fear is felt it is relieved, in the world of the song.

A friend of mine was an alcoholic, he knew it, his drinking was wrecking his life, wrecking his family, his wife was going to leave him, he couldn't stop. He tried and tried and kept on drinking. One day during a long drive heading north through empty Michigan countryside, he heard himself saying, out loud, "Jesus, Jesus, I can't carry this. *You* take it." And, he said, Jesus did take it, some kind of space opened and he was sober ever after.

That's Grace, obviously. My friend deeply knew himself to be a "wretch" as a drunkard. John Newton the reformed slave trader who wrote "Amazing Grace" was telling his own life story. But something else is happening in the opening line of the hymn as it performs what it describes, even for a relative non-wretch like me. There is a sense that prayer is itself the "answer" to prayer, and in just the same way, "Amazing Grace" becomes *operative*. When I say "Amazing Grace, how sweet the sound," the phrase "how sweet the sound" is at once self-reflective, meaning the sound of the words just said, just being said, and it also means the cosmic sound that is a divine emanation, a force one can feel entering one's body as it is invoked. Pythagorus and others have believed in the sacred music of the spheres. Buddhist philosophy speaks of a cosmic sound, "nada," that may be heard within in utter silence. Did the *sound* save a wretch like me? Just so, it is a paradox, and I have long thought that paradox is the only proper way to speak of the divine.

Beyond the mystery of Grace causing and relieving fear, I become engaged in the "I" of the hymn shifting to "we." We've come through a lot, with the help of Grace, and Grace "will bring us home." This brings us to the country of "Pilgrim's Progress," where the saved are gathered by the river they are about to cross. The final stanza's invocation of time, ten thousand years as a portion of an eternity spent in singing God's praise, is lifted into ecstasy by "bright shining as the sun," which may refer to what it is like "there," or to how brightly we ourselves will shine. Past, present, future, and finally eternity, become encompassed in brightness.

But it is the return of the refrain that I most truly embrace, or that embraces me. And how this can happen without a trace of Christian "belief" on my part is itself a mystery. Something to do with Coleridge's "suspension of disbelief," I suppose. Happily, this is not a mystery I feel any need to solve.

O God, Our Help in Ages Past

Our God, our help in ages past,
our hope for years to come,
our shelter from the stormy blast,
and our eternal home.

Under the shadow of Thy throne
Thy saints have dwelt secure;
sufficient is thine arm alone,
and our defense is sure.

Before the hills in order stood
or earth received its frame,
from everlasting thou art God,
to endless years the same.

A thousand ages in Thy sight
are like an ev'ning gone;
short as the watch that ends the night
before the rising sun.

Time, like an ever-rolling stream,
bears all its sons away;
they fly forgotten, as a dream
dies at the op'ning day.

Our God, our help in ages past,
our hope for years to come,
be thou our guide while life shall last,

and our eternal home!

Isaac Watts (1674–1748)

VIJAY SESHADRI

IMMANENCE

In her memoir fragment "A Sketch of the Past," Virginia Woolf says that until she wrote *To the Lighthouse* she was haunted by the memory of her mother, who had died when Woolf was thirteen. The writing of *To the Lighthouse*—Mrs. Ramsay, the main character, is based on Julia Stephen—was cathartic. It put the haunting to rest. Most writers understand the process. Memories, their mass bending and shaping inner space, exciting or oppressing the imagination, are suddenly given over through the act of writing to a mausoleum of words. They lose their force and their capacity to involve the psyche in themselves. Also, though, they lose their pungency and immediacy. Woolf implies that she felt relief and freedom when she put her memories to rest in her novel, but when I first experienced this catharsis I felt a sense of loss. The memory I purged by consigning it to the page was a painful one. Its stinging presence had been with me for so long, though, and revisiting it in my mind evoked the experience that it was a picture of so precisely, with such clarity and detail, that I was bereft when I realized that through its articulation its force had been drained.

I've written before about my first encounter with "O God, Our Help in Ages Past," and about the imprint the hymn left on my mind. That writing, curiously, hasn't drained the memory of its force or erased the imprint. The imprint in fact seems clearer and more deeply etched every time I visit the chamber in my mind where it is located. It has also taken on new properties over time, uncanny properties. It seems to glow, and it illumines more brilliantly the fragmentary images and sense memories that surround it—and, amazingly, it illuminates fresh images, images that I don't remember remembering before, but that I now remember.

What I wrote about the hymn almost twenty years ago comes from one of my own memoir fragments. It is part of a story about immigration and dislocation and fraught assimilation into a new culture. At the very end of the

1950s, my mother and I were fetched from India by my father—he had been in America getting his Ph.D. in physical chemistry—and taken to Ottawa, where he assumed a postdoctoral fellowship with Canada's National Research Council. The memoir fragment's relevant passage, part of a description of the neighborhood we found ourselves in, is this one:

> The people who lived around us were named Matherson, Campbell, Jones. Their religion was nonconformist and their game was ice hockey. I never took to the hockey, though I played a lot of it. I possessed a talent for the religion, though. My parents had the residual piety that characterizes even the most agnostic Indians of their generation, and a God-is-a-diamond-with-many-facets attitude toward doctrine. When the mother of a friend of mine asked if I could accompany him to Sunday school, they said yes, and I became a valued member of a Christian congregation. I might have been valued because I was seen as a heathen ripe for conversion, but I doubt it. Those people were generous and unintrusive and enlightened. They had a reticence and dignity appropriate to their climate and dispensation. I'm sure they liked me as much as they did because I was a loud and contented hymn-singer, and almost letter perfect in learning the Bible stories. My favorite story was the one about Joseph, who was depicted in our Bible reader wearing his coat of many colors while his jealous brothers circled around him, getting ready to throw him into the pit. My favorite hymn was "O God, Our Help in Ages Past," whose first stanza,

> O God our help in ages past,
> Our hope for years to come,
> Our shelter from the stormy blast,
> And our eternal home

still calls up for me an image of stick-like, barely discernible human figures toiling over an immense, featureless landscape.

This account, with its quick sketch of my parents, its understated ironies, and its details of social history, is not the account I would give now of this moment in my life. My father and my mother both passed away recently, and their deaths have not only left me alone with our once shared memories but altered the meaning of those memories. When I first told this story, I told it as if it were about our finding our way in a new world. If I told it today, I would dispense with society and with the social details. I would linger in the vision the hymn gave me, which in the aftermath of losing my parents seems to be suffused, mysteriously, with the love I have for them. I would paint a picture of that landscape, which is no longer featureless in my imagination. It seems, rather, like an immense flow of rust-brown igneous rock, scored and grooved and fissured with semicircles. And the sticklike figures, whom I see far below me, are now in my imagination recognizably ourselves.

My parents had made an immense leap of faith in coming to this continent when they did, when no one from their ancient South Indian world was ever disposed to leave it, especially to go so far, to a place so strange to their habits, understandings, their sense of social order. They had left one civilization for another and for long, suspenseful years were caught between two contrived human constructs, suspended over the abyss of reality. When I hear "O God, Our Help in Ages Past," when I spool it out in my mind, they seem somehow to live inside the hymn. The power of its petition seems to invest them with an absolute reality, and for my part I can almost feel myself in the middle of that leap of faith, in all its terror and exhilaration.

Jesus Is All the World to Me

Jesus is all the world to me,
my life, my joy, my all.
He is my strength from day to day,
without him I would fall.
When I am sad, to him I go,
no other one can cheer me so;
when I am sad, he makes me glad,
he's my friend.

Jesus is all the world to me,
my friend in trials sore.
I go to him for blessings, and
he gives them o'er and o'er:
He sends the sunshine and the rain;
he sends the harvest's golden grain;
sunshine and rain, harvest of grain,
he's my friend.

Jesus is all the world to me,
and true to him I'll be.
Oh, how could I this friend deny,
when he's so true to me?
Following him I know I'm right;
he watches o'er me day and night.
Following him by day and night,
he's my friend.

Jesus is all the world to me,
I want no better friend.
I trust him now, I'll trust him when

life's fleeting days shall end:
Beautiful life with such a friend,
beautiful life that has no end,
eternal life, eternal joy,
he's my friend.

Will L. Thompson (1847–1909)

PATRICIA JABBEH WESLEY

IN THE MIDST OF BOMBING AND WAR, I TURNED TO HYMNS

War has its own music. However tragic, like poetry, war has its own rhythms and its way of bringing us back to the music we used to know. But unlike poetry or a hymn, the music of war rises out of the explosion of bombed buildings, missile attacks, in the bombardment of early morning gun battles between warring factions, in ominous sounds of crumbling cities and in the shrill cries of the dying or soon to be executed. Such horror makes every organ in us tremble, that senselessness of human cruelty which is as inexplicable as an insane language. Ironically, for me, this horror turned me more to hymns, to songs and poetry, all of which are solemnly powerful, like the old hymns Mamma sang in our home when I was a child. In times of difficulty, we often turn to that old place where we have known our healing to come from. For my family, that old place was in the great hymns of the church. It was in that ugliness of the Liberian civil war, the starvation, desperation, and the constant fear of being killed that I rediscovered the power of the old hymns I grew up on. Everything else had failed us, so I needed to help my family find that old place of peace. As a poet, that decision came naturally.

One day in May, 1990, as war engulfed our country, I pulled one of our old family hymnals off a bookshelf and began to leaf through it. The news on the BBC radio was clear. Tens of thousands of rebels led by Liberian warlord Charles Taylor were drawing closer to Monrovia, our capital. They were fighting a guerrilla style war against Liberian government troops. Samuel K. Doe, the President of Liberia, was losing the battle every day. His army therefore turned on us civilians, and like the rebels, were also killing thousands of civilians throughout the country and across Monrovia and its suburbs.

The invading rebel army called itself The National Patriotic Front of Liberia or NPFL, but we civilians called them "rebels." They also nicknamed themselves Freedom Fighters, but we knew that they were guerrillas, looters, killers, and rapists. The news of the bloodbath and the devastation of our cities and villages on their way to Monrovia defined them and their rebel warfare for us.

Charles Taylor and his forces invaded Liberia from a northern border town in Nimba County on Christmas Eve, 1989. By May, 1990, they'd already captured most of the country in their mission to remove the Liberian government, and were moving fast toward the capital city where we lived. They'd leveled many cities and villages, and now foreign governments, including America, were evacuating their citizens from Liberia. There are no words to describe the desperation of a nation preparing to be overrun by such a powerful and unruly rebel army as the NPFL. Nor are there words to describe the aloneness we felt as the world suddenly abandoned us. In that same month of May, Charles Taylor's NPFL suffered a breakup and split into two warring factions, becoming the NPFL and the Independent National Patriotic Front of Liberia, or INPFL. The original NPFL was now at war to remove the Liberian President, Samuel K. Doe, and his government, even as they were locked in a fierce war against their breakaway group, the INPFL. The new rebel group, INPFL, led by Taylor's former fellow co-commander, Prince Y. Johnson, was also caught up in a similar two-battlefront-fight against Taylor and Doe.

All of this news was so overwhelming, I started writing poetry with a new dedication, writing about the encroaching war. But not even poetry could comfort me. I felt that our family needed something else to hang on to. We were devout Christians who held family devotions every morning and evening, and taught our children the values of Christ. Therefore, it was not difficult to think of needing a theme song or a hymn for our family. I thought we needed a song we could hide in our hearts if we needed to flee the city.

I sat on our terrazzo tiled living room floor that day, and found Will Thompson's "Jesus Is All the World to Me." The hymn would become my favorite hymn in the war. Singing it in the privacy of my bedroom one day as the war drew closer, I knew that this was the hymn for my family. I used to know the power of such old hymns as a little girl growing up in my mother's church during the 1960s. Even as a little girl, I was drawn to them as I was to poetry. Maybe I loved them because Mamma sang them out loud through the house when she was down. Maybe I loved them because they were my first contact with poetry. I had memorized many of them as a child, held them to heart, and believed in their power. This was the old place of peace, I thought, where I needed to take my family. This would be our healing.

When the war began on December 24, 1989, I was a young wife and mother of three small children, living with my family in Congo Town, a suburb of Monrovia. My husband Mlen-Too and I were on the faculty at the University of Liberia while volunteering to mentor and minister to university students throughout Liberia. As the war drew closer, we began looking for the tools we needed to help our family survive the carnage we knew was coming. We began making the kind of plans people who have never seen war think they can make. Our experience as Christian leaders in the community was important if we were to survive, we thought. By early June, 1990, the rebels were only about 30 miles east of Monrovia, but much closer to our home.

What does one do when their country is being overrun by two powerful and unruly rebel groups at war with a disorganized government army? What does one do when they cannot go to work, go to the bank, or take their children to school? What does one do when "all other ground is sinking sand," as fighters on all sides burn down villages and cities, killing tens of thousands, raping women and young girls, turning small boys into child soldiers, and blowing up everything in sight? By mid-June, we were surrounded on land, on sea, and in the air, in one of the world's most brutal civil wars. Troops loyal to Liberia's President, Samuel K. Doe, fought hard, but they were fast losing the war. Already tens of thousands of Liberians were dead. How would we survive the carnage? How could we survive? What would we take with us if we had to run and what would we leave behind? Would we take our hymnals, our Bibles, our books, our clothes, food, or would we be forced to run with only the clothes on our backs?

After I decided on "Jesus Is All the World to Me," I quickly memorized all the verses, and gave the hymnal to my husband to do the same. Then we helped our small children learn the words by singing the hymn in our daily morning and evening devotions. The children—Besie-Nyesuah, seven years old; Mlen-Too II, or MT, four; and my brother, Wyne, who lived with us, twelve years old—needed to learn the song as well. Our third child, Gee, a boy, was only eight months old, so he only looked on as we sang the hymn over and over, along with other songs we also needed to memorize. At first, the three children were slow to learn it, but soon they could sing one or two of the verses without looking in the hymnal. In addition to preparing our immediate family, we also needed to help my aging mother and her two teenage boys understand what we were doing. They had moved in with us due to the fighting. After some difficulty, Mamma was singing along. "Jesus Is All the World to Me" was not among her favorites, nor was she familiar with it. She was a Pentecostal whose old-time favorites were songs like "What a Friend We Have in Jesus," "When We All Get to Heaven," and "There's Power in the Blood."

The words of the hymn took on a new meaning for me as my family and I journeyed through the war. There is something powerful in a hymn that confirms our hopes and belief in the God who is not only our Lord in a time of peace, but also in a time of war. I examined the words of this great hymn like a poet examines the lines of their own poem before publication. I explored the words as they became one of my weapons on our painful journey. I studied the words as though they were the gospel that I needed to carry me through the long military roadblocks, the horrors of walking through the jungle with my family as we fled our home on August 1, 1990, through intimidation from the rebels and government soldiers, on our long walk into Charles Taylor's rebel stronghold to flee the fighting that would break out in our neighborhood a week after our flight. I was the custodian of what I knew as *our* hymn, so my family would stay strong.

"Jesus is all the world to me, / my life, my joy, my all; / He is my strength from day to day, / without Him I would fall. / When I am sad, to Him I go, / no other one can cheer me so; / when I am sad, He makes me glad, / He's my Friend," we sang. If Jesus was all the world to me, and if he was my life, my joy, my all, then it did not matter whether I survived the war or not, whether my family survived or not, whether we starved to death or not, I told myself daily.

But it was also important to know that because Jesus was all the world to me, and because he was my friend in this time of tremendous pain, he would keep my family safe. He would be our strength, our hope, our fortress, the one and only one who knew us in our deepest pain and in our greatest joy. I took every word and every line and every verse to heart, and claimed it, with many other hymns. If my world was falling apart, if my world was devastated, as it was in 1990 and 1991, through the violence, as we were tortured and faced death every day, then there was nothing to worry about as long as "Jesus was all the world to me."

The power of a hymn, whether one is a poet or not, is rooted in faith and in the belief that we have God, the creator of the universe, who gave his all for us on the cross. This hymn explores that faith. As a Christian, my faith in the Bible's validity and in the truth that Christ brings, helps me believe in the power of the words of that hymn. Will Thompson wrote, "I trust Him now, I'll trust Him when / life's fleeting days shall end," and I claim the words for myself. These words are more meaningful to me in a way than the words of my poems could ever be. Yes, I have written poetry that explores my painful war experiences, and many of my poems can bring an audience to tears when I read. But the words of a hymn carry more power than that. There is that sacredness in the words of a hymn that is more powerful than the words of a poem. Words like "Jesus is all the world to me, / my Friend in trials sore; / I go to Him for blessings, / and He gives them o'er and o'er" are based on the Bible, and we Christians believe in the holiness of the Bible. It was that faith, in the Bible, and in that hymn, that sustained my family and me through the Liberian civil war. In that faith, we had hope that there is a great God, who makes all wars cease, the God who gives grace to the desolate refugee of war. Jesus is all the world to me.

CONTRIBUTORS

Kaveh Akbar was born in Tehran, Iran. He founded and edits *Divedapper*, a website of interviews with leading voices in contemporary poetry. His poems have appeared in *Poetry*, *Tin House*, *American Poetry Review*, *Narrative*, *Guernica*, and elsewhere. He teaches in the MFA program at Purdue.

Zeina Hashem Beck is a Lebanese poet with degrees from the American University of Beirut. She won the 2016 May Sarton New Hampshire Poetry Prize for her second full-length collection, *Louder than Hearts*.

Scott Cairns is Curator's Distinguished Professor at University of Missouri, founding director Writing Programs in Greece, and director of the creative writing program at Seattle Pacific University. In addition to eight books of poems, he has published translations, essays, and a spiritual memoir.

Roy Carroll Professor of Honors Arts and Sciences, and Director of the Center for Jewish Studies at the University of North Carolina Asheville, Richard Chess has published four books of poems. An innovative teacher, he explores methods of contemplative pedagogy in his work with college students.

Professor of English and director of creative writing at Vanderbilt, Kate Daniels was born in Richmond, Virginia and has degrees from the University of Virginia and Columbia University. In addition to awards and prizes she has received for her poetry, Professor Daniels is a leading voice for the use of art in medicine.

Kwame Dawes is Chancellor's Professor of English and Editor-in-Chief of *Prairie Schooner* at University of Nebraska. Born in Ghana, he spent his childhood and early adulthood in Jamaica. A prolific and celebrated writer of poetry, fiction, nonfiction, and plays, he also collaborates with musicians and with filmmakers and visual artists.

Margaret Gibson has published eleven books of poetry and a memoir about growing up in Richmond, Virginia. She has been writer in residence at schools and universities across the country, most recently, Professor in Residence at University of Connecticut. She lives in Preston, Connecticut.

Dana Gioia is the Poet Laureate of California. He is the author of five collections of poetry, including *Interrogations at Noon* (2001), which won the American Book Award, and *99 Poems: New & Selected* (2016), which won the Poets' Prize. He is the former Chairman of the National Endowment for the Arts.

Lorna Goodison divides her time between her native Jamaica and the University of Michigan, where she is Professor Emerita of English Language and Literature, and Professor Emerita of Afroamerican and African Studies. One of the leading West Indian writers of her generation, she is also a painter.

Jason Gray is the author of *Photographing Eden*, winner of the 2008 Hollis Summers Prize. He has also published two chapbooks, *How to Paint the Savior* and *Adam & Eve Go to the Zoo*. His poems have appeared in *Poetry*, *The American Poetry Review*, *The Kenyon Review*, *Literary Imagination*, *Poetry Ireland Review*, and other places.

Linda Gregerson is the Caroline Walker Bynum Distinguished University Professor of English Language and Literature at the University of Michigan, where she teaches Renaissance literature and creative writing. Recipient of many honors and awards, she is a current Chancellor of the Academy of American Poets.

Robert Hass is a California poet and environmental activist. He served two terms as Poet Laureate of the United States, and is a past Chancellor of the American Academy of Poets. Among his many awards and honors are a Pulitzer Prize and a National Book Award.

Poet, teacher, and tireless advocate for poetry, Edward Hirsch is president of the John Simon Guggenheim Memorial Foundation. From 2009–2014 he served as a Chancellor of the Academy of American Poets. His 1991 book *How to Read a Poem and Fall in Love with Poetry* was a national bestseller.

Jay Hopler was born in San Juan, Puerto Rico. A poet, essayist, and translator, he is a professor of English at the University of Southern Florida. He won the Yale Younger Poet's prize, the oldest continuously running literary prize in America. Together with his wife, Kimberly Johnson, he edited *Before the Door of God: An Anthology of Devotional Poetry*.

Mark Jarman is the author of numerous poetry collections, including *The Heronry* and *Bone Fires: New and Selected Poems*, both from Sarabande Books. He has also published two books of essays about poetry, *The Secret of Poetry* and *Body and Soul: Essays on Poetry*. He is Centennial Professor of English at Vanderbilt University.

Kimberly Johnson is a poet, teacher, and scholar with wide-ranging interests. Professor of English at Brigham Young University, she teaches courses in British literature and has published books of poems, scholarly work on sixteenth- and seventeenth-century lyric poetry, and translations from Greek and Latin.

A New England outdoorsman and man of letters, Sydney Lea was Poet Laureate of Vermont from 2011–2015. His many books of poems, fiction, and nonfiction draw on his rural roots. He founded *New England Review* and has taught at Dartmouth, Yale, Wesleyan, and Middlebury.

Originally from Kingston, Jamaica, Shara McCallum is the author of five books of poetry, published in the US and UK. For over ten years she was the Director of the Stadler Center for Poetry at Bucknell University. She now teaches creative writing & literature at Penn State University.

Award-winning Kentucky poet Maurice Manning has published six volumes of poems. He has degrees from Earlham College, University of Alabama, and University of Kentucky. He teaches English and creative writing at Transylvania University and lives on a farm in Washington County, Kentucky.

Kathleen Norris's books of poems and essays take a wide view of Christian practice. Raised in Methodist and UCC churches, currently she is a member of a Presbyterian church in her mother's home town in South Dakota, a member of an Episcopal church in Honolulu, and an oblate of a Benedictine monastery in North Dakota.

Yehoshua November teaches at Rutgers University and Touro College. He is the author of two collections of poems, *Two Worlds Exist*, a finalist for The National Jewish Book Award in Poetry and The Paterson Poetry Prize, and *God's Optimism*, which won the Main Street Rag Poetry Book Award and was a finalist for the *LA Times* Book Prize. He lives with his family in Teaneck, New Jersey,

Born in Philadelphia, Jacqueline Osherow has degrees from Harvard-Radcliffe, where she wrote for the Harvard Lampoon, and from Princeton University. She has published seven books of poems. She is Distinguished Professor in the Department of English at The University of Utah.

Author of sixteen collections of poetry, most recently *Waiting for the Light*, Alicia Ostriker describes herself as a "third-generation atheist socialist Jew." She has written extensively about Jewish scripture and tradition, and she leads midrash-writing workshops in her New York City apartment. She is currently a Chancellor of the Academy of American Poets.

Born in Bangalore, India, and raised in Columbus, Ohio where his father taught chemistry at Ohio State University, Vijay Seshadri lives in Brooklyn and is a professor at Sarah Lawrence College. In 2014 he became the first Asian

American to win the Pulitzer Prize in poetry for his book, *3 Sections*.

In 1991 Patricia Jabbeh Wesley and her family came through the Liberian Civil War to a new life in America. The author of five volumes of award-winning poems, Wesley is an advocate for justice and reconciliation of people in conflict. She teaches English and Creative Writing at Pennsylvania State University.

ACKNOWLEDGMENTS AND PERMISSIONS

Thank you to Fr. C. Raymond Selker, OFM, and to Rev. Dr. Stephanie May for their assistance when this book was just an idea. Thank you to the directors and staff of the Louisville Institute, and to my colleagues there, for financial support that made the project possible, and for comments and criticisms that improved the outcome of it.

Robert Hass' piece on "O Little Town of Bethlehem" appeared in *The Washington Post* as part of his Poet's Choice series when he was Poet Laureate of the United States from 1995–1997. It is reprinted here with the author's permission.

Versions of the essays appearing in this book were originally published in the following venues:

Commonweal: "A Catholic Love for a Protestant Hymn" by Maurice Manning

First Things: "Babel Was My Hometown: Singing the 'Tantum Ergo' in '60s L.A." by Dana Gioia

Harvard Divinity Bulletin: "One Bread: One Body: One Love" by Kate Daniels, "'Great is Thy Faithfulness': A Meditation" by Kwame Dawes, "'Silent Night'" by Jason Gray, "'Come, My Beloved, to Greet the Bride'" by Yehoshua November, and "I Love to Tell the Story" by Kathleen Norris

Image: "Was There a Speaker on the Building Opposite Us?" by Zeina Hashem Beck, "'Be Thou My Vision'" by Scott Cairns, "'Immortal, Invisible, God only Wise'" by Lorna Goodison, "'O Come, O Come, Emmanuel'" by Linda Gregerson, "Caedmon's Hymn" by Edward Hirsch, "Short Treatise on Slowing Down" by Sydney Lea, "Three Verses from Hallel" by Jacqueline Osherow, and "'Amazing Grace': Singer and Song" by Alicia Ostriker

Literary Hub: "Learning to Pray, Learning to Write" by Kaveh Akbar

ABOUT THE EDITOR

Jeffrey L. Johnson studied at St. Olaf College, Yale Divinity School, and Boston University, and he is the author of *Harbors of Heaven: Bethlehem and the Places We Love* and *Acquainted with Night: The Shadow of Death in Contemporary Poetry*. He has received the Thomas Merton Foundation Poetry of the Sacred Award, and his poems and essays have appeared in *The Christian Century, First Things, Christianity and Literature, Anglican Theological Review, Encounter,* and *The Mars Hill Review.*

ABOUT ORISON BOOKS

Orison Books is a 501(c)3 non-profit literary press focused on the life of the spirit from a broad and inclusive range of perspectives. We seek to publish books of exceptional poetry, fiction, and non-fiction from perspectives spanning the spectrum of spiritual and religious thought, ethnicity, gender identity, and sexual orientation.

As a non-profit literary press, Orison Books depends on the support of donors. To find out more about our mission and our books, or to make a donation, please visit www.orisonbooks.com.